a memoir

FOSTERED

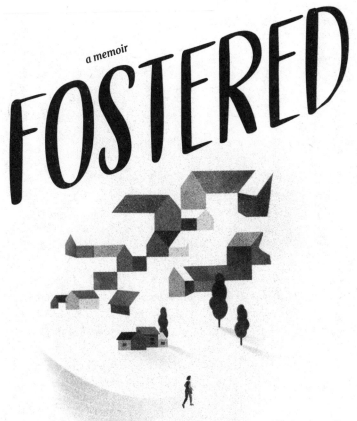

One Woman's Powerful Story of Finding
Faith and Family through Foster Care

TORI HOPE PETERSEN

B&H
PUBLISHING
NASHVILLE, TENNESSEE

Published by B&H Publishing Group
Nashville, Tennessee

Dewey Decimal Classification: 306.874
Subject Heading: FOSTER CHILDREN / FOSTER HOME CARE
/ CHRISTIAN LIFE

Unless otherwise noted all Scripture is taken from the New
International Version®, NIV® Copyright ©1973, 1978, 1984, 2011 by
Biblica, Inc.® Used by permission. All rights reserved worldwide.

Scripture references marked ESV are taken from the English Standard
Version. ESV® Text Edition: 2016. Copyright © 2001 by Crossway
Bibles, a publishing ministry of Good News Publishers.

Cover design and illustration by Bárbara Tamilin /
Illustration (USA) Inc. Author photo by Lizzie Meyer.

2 3 4 5 6 • 26 25 24 23 22

To my babies, Leyonder, Sar, Ezzeri, and the ones who are not yet in my home. God placed you in my heart before I even knew you. You've been my motivation to build a life of zealous love. Every day you inspire me to love deeper yet softer.

To Scott. You became my dad when an entire town advised you to wash your hands of me. By not listening to them, you've granted me a lifetime of being heard.

To my mama. My hero who granted me life, engraved in me wild determination, and raised me to embody grit and generosity.

To Tonya. My mother figure, minister, best friend, and mentor. Your gentleness and hospitality are forever embedded in me.

To Jacob, my husband. I'm not sure if this should be a thank-you as much as it should be an apology for all the secondhand trauma you've experienced as I continue to discover who God has made me to be. Thank you for holding space for me and loving me. I love all of you with all of me.

To God, who has gifted me this messy and stunning life to draw me closer to You. I am Your daughter.

CONTENTS

AUTHOR'S NOTE

This story has forced me to wade into deep waters. I do not hang out where it is shallow, but sometimes I've needed to swim back to shore to catch my breath from the winds and waves that have come as a result of being born into this life. Thankfully, throughout this story, a Lifeguard found me, and with Him I've come to appreciate the depths of the ocean and the storm. It's where I sleep.

But I'd never throw you into the deep waters without support, so you should know, as you read, that you'll hit big waves, dark nights, and hail that feels as if it'll never let up. There are moments in the journey you'll want to shield yourself with an umbrella. And for some, you might need to do just that. Having been through some terrible times, and not enjoying when my brain unexpectedly reawakens my memory, I always appreciate when a book or a movie offers a *trigger warning*.

So here is yours: if you've been through family abuse or trauma, if you've been through your own foster care saga and you're not quite ready to relive certain parts, or if you're in an especially tender season for some other reason, now is the moment I give you the permission to choose if *right now* is the best time to sail your ship into these deep waters. It's not that everything in this book is stormy—it's not. There is hope, and in this story you will find the Lifeguard who saved me will be by *your* side too as you wade. You too can become a storm sleeper. But I owe you the truth that the joy, love, and victory found in these pages comes against a backdrop of pain, sorrow, and darkness.

You may find you aren't ready to explore the path ahead, but if you are, let's start here.

First, the cover of this book says "memoir," and it is one, but not in the ways you might expect. It doesn't go through every nook and cranny of my story—it's not a "play by play." Rather, it's a collection of selected vignettes that give you the impression of the whole.

Second, the stories and opinions you read are mine and mine alone. I do not represent the story, nor the opinion, of every youth who has experienced foster care. I am one story among many.

Third, my prayer over this book has been Genesis 50:20. In my own story, I have seen that all that was intended to harm me, God intended for good to accomplish what is now being done—the saving of many lives. And my prayer is that as you witness this in my journey, you'll see the same thing in your own story.

Fourth, my intention for this book is Mark 16:15—my greatest hope being that I am an obedient witness of Love, and this is one way that I might fulfill the command of going into all the world and preach not just my story, but the gospel to all creation. It is the gospel that saved me, again and again and again. It is the gospel that keeps me.

Ultimately, I've written this book, not so you can see what God did through me, but so that you will believe what God can do through you, no matter the odds.

CREATED

My first memory happened before I was born. Or maybe I can't claim it to be my own memory but a first-person interpretation of the story Mom told me. When it comes to memories, we can't be sure, even of our own perspective. What I am sure about is what we remember and how we remember it influences our perceptions about ourselves, others, and all our other memories.

Symbols flashed positive for pregnancy and HIV. Despite AIDs poisoning her body and her lack of religiosity, my mom prayed over my life. Realizing the impossibility of erasing the times she fell asleep in places she should have been keenly aware, she felt regret snuggled next to me in the pit of her stomach.

Her friends stood shocked when she told them about her pregnancy, especially those who knew heartbreak because of the inability to conceive. Conception through rape seemed absurd. Mom spent her night at the wrong place at the right time of the month to discover me in her womb weeks later. A friend heard her cry and sent a card that read, "'For I know the plans I have for you,' declares the LORD, 'plans to prosper you and not to harm you, plans to give you hope and a future'" Jer. 29:11 NIV). She rubbed her belly, feeling me swim in her amniotic fluid, aware HIV infected her blood. She took another pill hoping the medicine would prevent me from catching the virus, and she prayed, "God, You may not have a future and hope for me, but I pray a victorious future for this baby."

I was born healthy and HIV negative. Expecting Mom to die before labor, the doctor tested her again. Symbols flashed negative for HIV. The doctor determined the first test a false positive. Declaring miracles in the medical industry would put medicine out of business. Mom saw it as a sign of victory and hope—Victoria Hope. I qualify the mishap as a miracle that God has made of my life.

Hours of counseling and parenting classes Mom willingly attended played a large part in me "turning out okay." Many heroes played a role in my being where I am now, but Mom was my first hero. More than anyone else wanted me to make it, she did.

Jailed in Harris County for solicitation of prostitution, Mom heard my heartbeat and saw my hands laying under my head on the ultrasound. She said ever since she saw me, she loved me more than anything she'd ever loved before, and she never ceased to let me know.

Transported from the jail, my mom labored in the back of a police car. Handcuffed to the hospital bed, Mom delivered me. Falcon, a man who started out as a trick, took me for three days until Mom was released. She never stopped telling me and everyone else that I was the most beautiful girl there ever was.

~ * * * ~

From a young age, Mom made clear that men took care of us and told me that one of the smartest things I could do for myself was marry a rich man. I could have never anticipated how antsy this would make me when I began to date, hoping my boyfriends and their parents wouldn't assume I was interested in a relationship for the money, since every boy I could have dated would most definitely inherit more than me.

Mom would say, "Jack takes good care of us." In the mornings she woke up to a wad of cash resting in a crystal bowl on her bedside table. It was provided by Jack to keep Mom "grounded." As I understood it, Jack was my father, and I called him "Dad." He sat me on his lap while he played the grand piano in our living room.

Mom and Jack were sleeping in the morning I turned my head from Scooby Doo toward the loud crash. Our door swung open and uniformed men busted through our front door and quickly scattered throughout our house. Cabinets and drawers flung open as the officers searched.

A man shook a gallon-sized plastic zip bag in my face. "Do you know what this is?"

Plenty of times before this day, I went through a training with Mom. It consisted of loyalties to her and a hate for law enforcement. Pointing out cop cars in traffic and policemen in uniform, she convincingly trained me: "Cops are bad. If cops ask us anything, we say nothing. Cops want to take you to bad places, away from Mommy." It was almost instinctual for me to shake my head no at the police officer, even though I knew what was in the bag.

Men and women of color fear for their lives because video cameras have shown policemen and women abusing their power, but we might consider that the poor and communities of color also fear for their lives in the face of law enforcement because people they love and trust tell them to.

It took me some time to understand that not all men with badges would abuse their power by pushing me around and slamming me into a police car after experiencing this at seventeen years old in the foster care system. As a young adult and foster mom, I'd learn many of those uniformed men Mom and the media said were bad actually intended to keep little girls like me safe.

A woman who wasn't so scary gently moved toward me and picked me up to place me on her hip just like Mom did. We walked from the front of the living room to the back door—in between was the kitchen, where flour and sugar were ripped out of the cabinets and poured onto the counters. Mom was on her knees. She shook on the kitchen floor crying, "My baby. My baby." The gun in the police officer's hand pointed toward her.

The soft lady swept right past the scene as if it wasn't even happening. She sat me on my swing set and explained to me that I was going to leave for some time while Mom got better.

~ * * * ~

After the house was raided, the policemen were silent, and I sat on a metal floor in the back of a dark-colored truck shaped like a box until I was eventually transferred to a car that took me to Sue's. Sue was an older woman who fostered many girls, and everything in her house was notably neat. She had a pool in her backyard that shined blue, and she promised if we ate all of our food we could swim in the pool.

The mac and cheese Sue served looked like smashed corn someone spit in, and her peanut butter and jelly sandwiches were so repulsive to me that when I tried to eat them I gagged and spit them out.

With the manners Mom taught me, I asked if I could have crab legs, steak, or green beans. I said please persistently, but neither Sue nor I would relent. She refused to cook me crab legs, and I refused to eat her noodles doused in butter and cheese.

While it is common for youth to enter foster care thinking there will not be enough food because they were without food before, that wasn't my case. Mom's drug money paid for high dining meals. I had never eaten *this kind* of food. I rarely ate while at Sue's, and I watched the other girls swim often.

~ * * * ~

I slept on the bottom bunk of one of several beds in one room. All of us girls had matching red sheets and red fleece blankets. I didn't pee the bed at home, but all of a sudden my dreams depicted me falling off cliffs into deep waters.

In the morning, Sue hurried me as I stripped the soiled bedding to drop them down the shoot. After the bed was bare, Sue wrapped her hand around my arm to march me to the bathroom. I'd take my underwear off to "wash" and ring them out in the toilet. The residue from the white porcelain came off onto my garments, and I scrubbed until Sue said I could stop.

I continued to pee the bed, and though it made no difference, Sue punished me the same every time. My foster sister who slept above me noticed my sheets were wet again on a morning Sue was out. As she stood above my bed, fear consumed my four-year-old body. I remained in bed because I knew getting out of it would bring me over the toilet bowl. As my breaths got quicker, the teenage girl gently rubbed my shoulders to comfort me. "Help me take the sheets off." She said as she quickly balled the sheets into her arms and handed them to me.

I followed her as she walked me down the long and narrow hallway to the laundry room. That evening I came back to my room where my bed was made for me. My sheets were clean. And from that day forward, I never woke up with wet sheets again.

It is now common knowledge that bed-wetting can occur when a child feels emotionally stressed or experiences traumatic events. But what is not as commonly known is how we can combat this trauma.

With just one try, my foster sister directly contradicted against my trauma, against what I expected and what I was used to. With just one try she transformed the imprints from Sue, and with one try I was healed. We have power to transform trauma, to minimize it, deepen it, or be a part of its healing.

If we want to diminish trauma, we must contradict trauma.

Now, hear me loud and clear: though I've dealt with my trauma in some of the healthiest ways a person can, the ghosts of my past life still haunt me.

I'm not saying we must try to verbally contradict a person who says she has experienced trauma, as if to convince her that her wounds aren't real by some nice speech or, worse, some sort of guilt trip. What I mean by *contradict trauma* is that we must act in ways that are opposite of the ways the wounds were inflicted on a person. Where trauma comes through vessels that are cruel and cold, we can be vessels of mercy and warmth. We can contradict the ways of trauma with the ways of Christ—the Man I'd soon come to know.

Chapter 2

IGNORED

As my caseworker drove me to my weekly visit with Mom, I looked out the window and imagined me and Mom tiptoeing across the barricades that divided the highway from the houses. Mom and I hopped down and up to each section. There was no Jersey Barrier I couldn't climb or drop to. I'd just grow longer legs or take the leap, extending my hand out to Mom so she could join me.

"Excuse me," I said, to make sure my caseworker was paying attention to me. He looked back at me startled. I'm not sure if his look was because he was surprised I was speaking up in the first place or because a four-year-old who came from a drug house had been taught such good manners.

I explained to my caseworker what happened at Sue's. While Melanie and I were playing a game where she jumped over me and then she rolled on the floor and I jumped over her, I accidentally fell on her while jumping. Melanie went upstairs and told Sue, and Sue came downstairs and she told Melanie to walk on my tummy. I clenched my stomach as tight as I could, but it didn't stop Melanie's feet from pressing into my gut, smooshing my body into the basement floor.

I stared at the back of my caseworker's head waiting for him to respond. After longer than he should have taken, he finally said that there was nothing he could do about it. I turned my head to look back out the window. I watched the cars zip the other way and imagined me and Mom together again dancing in the street, strutting between the cars, and walking on the big cement beams that prevented cars from colliding.

~ ✳ ✳ ~

Judging eyes pierced Mom as she read books to me on the cold tile floor at the social services office. I'd lay my head on her chest. Her hands brushed across my face. Occasionally a tear would drop on my forehead. She promised me we would be reunited soon and *this* would never happen again.

"Eskimo kisses," we'd say at the same time, bringing our faces close to one another. Her nose is an adult-sized version of mine, and though we share the same colored eyes as well, Mom's were bloodshot stained-glass windows. Raindrops collected on her sills when she brought her nose to touch and softly rub against mine, the same way I now brush my nose on my son's and daughter's.

~ ✳ ✳ ~

It felt like I had lived at Sue's for years, but Mom swore only months had gone by. My child years became as memorable as any others' after I gladly moved back in with Mom. We moved from the city to Mom's small hometown, which would become my hometown—Defiance, Ohio.

Jack's existence dissipated. Mom made clear, loudly and often, that it was Jack's fault I was ever taken away, and Mom couldn't risk people taking me away from her ever again. The skill I learned here was one I'd grow into for the rest of my life—move on from those you love without saying goodbye.

After Daddy Jack was Daddy Isaac, who couldn't have been much better than Daddy Jack since Mom and Isaac spent some time in jail together. Somehow Mom arranged it so I didn't go into the foster care system but lived with her friend, Pat. Nonetheless, Mom married Daddy Isaac. This would be the first wedding I'd attend outside of the womb. During Mom's first wedding, she was pregnant with me.

An immigrant man had paid Mom to marry him so he could enter the country. She was only married to him for a short time, which would make people suspicious that they only married for him to enter the country. Though that was the case, and it was illegal to do so, Mom swore it was the best financial option for our family at the time. And to make the marriage appear legit, she gave me the immigrant man's last name: "Abdul."

Mom picked out dresses for me to wear nearly every day, so the pink floral dress I wore for the rehearsal and the satin white dress I wore to be the flower girl both felt casual. My nose sniffed wide open flowers as a photographer took pictures of me. I pressed my fingers into the buds not yet bloomed, forcing them to open their eyes.

The wedding guests sat inside our living room, and though there was no airflow, Mom and Isaac struggled to light their unity candle. Ironically, each flame took turns burning out. Mom laughed, not knowing the candles accurately symbolized the rest of their marriage.

The reception was held at a local bar called the Wagon Wheel. Wedding guests sang karaoke until their words slurred and voices rasped. Isaac swept me off my feet and onto the dance floor. His fingers grasped my hands in his, and he swung me around the dance floor. His grip was strong, and his eyes crinkled into folds. His skin was dark, like he'd seen as much sun as he did shadows. Swinging his head back, he sang loud. I squealed, happy he was my new daddy.

He smiled so big, his eyes squinted into the shape of smiles. Three smiles on one face.

I giggled the kind of giggle any daughter would when dancing with her Father.

~ * * * ~

Not too many months later, a few ladies from my collection of porcelain dolls shattered against the wall when Mom accused Isaac of cheating on her with the neighbor, the babysitter, and any other woman with breath in her lungs. Mom's words seeped into the ceiling until the plaster began to rot.

My belongings, being the least valuable, were often the sacrifices broken. By the second grade, I'd had two hamster cages containing two different hamsters destroyed. One was an accident. Isaac fell on it while drunk and yelling at Mom for being a more successful businessperson than him. The other one was intentional. He picked up the glass container and slammed it on the ground. It was as if a bomb of hamster feces, wood chips, and glass shards exploded in our small two-bedroom apartment.

My greatest concern was my hamster, whom I named Cuddles. Neither Mom nor Isaac cared to help me find him. While I restlessly searched, they continued to scream at each other.

For as long as I can remember, I've had a thing for running away when I felt unseen, with the hope that people would chase me. Like maybe if my presence wasn't noticed, my absence would be.

The street we lived on was busy enough for me to believe I could catch a ride at the age of five, so I left during the fight and walked alongside the street with my thumb sticking out, the same way I'd seen the strangers Mom occasionally picked up catch a ride.

Tired of walking, I decided to sit but kept my thumb held high. After no one offered me a ride and Mom and Isaac didn't come looking for me, I felt a crushing weight. I thought maybe Mom had called the police to look for me. Even though she didn't like cops, I assumed she'd be desperate to find me. But when I walked back to the house to announce myself, the lights were dark and my parents were asleep. The crushing weight that I thought would be lifted was affirmed and would follow me as an adult. No one seemed to care where I was.

~ * * * ~

I'm not sure where Mom went, but when she left, Isaac laid towels out on the roof. We bathed in the sun, maybe trying to make up for the dusk we lived in. I could feel my skin burning. It hurt, but Isaac usually told me when to flip, so I waited a little longer before I spoke up.

He encouraged me to push through it a little longer because it'd make me stronger.

I lay on the towel in silence. The sun burned my back while the shingles felt like they scorched through the towel on my tummy. I reminded myself of the strength I'd have when it was over.

When Isaac finally gave me permission to turn over, he glanced at me surprised and cursed. "What kind of black person burns like that?" I didn't know what a black person meant or why a black person might not burn, but I became skeptical about the goodness of the sun.

~ * * * ~

I often escaped Mom and Isaac's quarrels by playing with the girls next door and across the street. Mom prohibited me from going into anyone's home—telling me stories of being a teen girl and living in a man's house who trafficked her—so we played outside. I played in Felicia's backyard the most.

We took turns burying each other from neck to toe in the sandbox, wiggling to see how much we could move before the little cracks emerged through the sand mold. Then we built sandcastles with grit between our fingers.

Felicia asked me if I wanted to come inside her house to see her pet bunny. Without hesitation she stood up and started walking inside, and with much hesitation I followed her. Though I knew I wasn't supposed to go inside, I knew it'd only be for a short time.

We quickly looked at the bunny cage and went back outside to play. I jumped when I heard my Mom's scream. "Victoria Hope!"

It seemed as if Mom had me over her knee before I walked through the door, but somehow we ended up on the couch. She screamed, with tears rolling down her face, "I told you not to ever go into anyone's house!" My bum became a drum. As she brought one hand to my bottom, she lifted the other. "Repeat after me!" She held me down by squeezing her leg on top of my back and shoulders. Her hands were a force. Her trauma continued screaming, and her fears continued to roll down her face in the form of tears. "I will not go into anyone else's house!" I repeated while sobbing and clenching my bottom. She let me go. I crawled onto the floor, but she demanded I stand up. My legs and backside quivered. I was jello and fragile.

She screamed at Isaac to take me upstairs.

He grabbed my arm and dragged me up the stairs. I tried to walk by myself, but my back ached and my legs shook. Once we got to the top of the stairs, Isaac picked me up and brought my face close to his. I didn't think I could bear whatever would happen next.

Isaac's breath mixed with mine. Then he whispered, "When I hit the mattress, start screaming." We looked at each other, sharing the hurt Mom caused. My body felt alleviation. My anxiety took respite. My giggles hid in between each fabricated scream.

~ * * * ~

Odds-and-ends jobs, getting paid under the table, and a boss that didn't mind me being around was the kind of work Mom took. Being a stay-at-home mom or a take-your-kid-to-work mom was her priority because it allowed her to stay close to me. Recalling the memories of being trafficked as a fourteen-year-old, she swore she could never let anyone hurt me the same way people hurt her.

I helped Mom work at a motel on the other side of town, right off of the interstate. She let me help strip the stained sheets off beds. My favorite job was spinning around as I sprayed air freshener to mask the odor.

On rare occasions, we went to the motel at night. Together, we'd watch a bit of television, and then she'd announce that it was time for her to leave.

"Don't open the door for anyone and keep the door locked." Mom kissed me goodbye, tested the lock, and wiggled the knob to make sure the lock was secure. "If anyone comes through the door, run. Do you understand?" I nodded my head, though I didn't know where I would run to, and I wasn't sure if I'd be fast enough.

My anxiety came at a young age. Some days it feels like it has only increased; other days it feels like a miracle that it isn't worse or that I'm not worse.

Mom closed the door, and I walked behind her to assure the door locked. Afraid to turn my back to the door, I slowly walked backward to sit on the bed. Mom left the television on for me to watch, but I wanted to make sure if anyone came in, I'd hear them, so I turned down the volume.

My tiredness grew heavier, and when my eyes shut, I shot them open. I hopped off the bed and walked backward to the part of the room farthest from the exit. I sprinted toward the door, came to an abrupt stop, and then walked backward, repeating the series of events.

I'd be ready to run.

Chapter 3

SACRIFICED

I don't know how many times we moved houses, but I know we moved frequently. The most memorable move happened after we came home at night and our house had been robbed. The big-screen television, wedding china, furniture, and many other valuables were gone.

Pieces of "grown-up conversations'" informed me that a drug deal had gone wrong. I'm not sure whether someone snitched or money was owed, but we left the house that night and never went back.

Following that move, more "grown-up conversations" informed me that Mom couldn't afford rent. Moving trucks were parked in the driveway when I returned home from school, and if I ever asked where we were going, I usually got a terse answer from Isaac like, "Somewhere else." My suspicion is that at times we didn't have a known next destination. It was only known that we had to leave.

Once, we found ourselves at a duplex in Jackson, Michigan; and I started attending school at Frost Elementary while Mom and Isaac sold vacuum cleaners called Kirbys.

I'd already attended a handful of elementary schools by the time I was in the third grade, but I hadn't noticed people having different shades of skin until I attended Frost. I also didn't notice the segregation until a brown girl named Princ'ss marched up to me on the playground and stuck her finger in the middle of my chest. Her head moved back and forth with the words she spoke. "You should be hanging out with the black girls."

I looked around and noticed the white girls playing on the swing set together, while the black girls choreographed cheers in the middle of the gravel track. The black girls were playing with black girls, and *I* hung out with the white girls.

She continued to move her head back and forth and point her finger at me. "You are a black girl. Black girls hang out with black girls. White girls hang out with white girls."

"I'm not black." I dangled out my arm in front of her as if she couldn't already see my honey-toned skin, but she abruptly slapped down my wrist.

Princ'ss grabbed my hair. "You have black girl hair. You are black."

I pulled my hair from her hand and started shaking my head back and forth too. "My Mom is white and she has curly hair."

"Your hair isn't curly. It's nappy. And you're dumb." She flicked my forehead and walked away.

My scalp ached whenever Mom brushed my hair. She didn't know what products to use or how to get through my curls without breaking them. She didn't have any resources that are readily accessible to transracial parents today, but she tried. As she detangled each knot, I told her what Princ'ss said as if I was tattling.

Mom said, "You do not have black-girl hair," with no more explanation. And more than ever, Mom tried to flatten my frizz.

Throughout my little-girl years, there'd be a lot of attempts to relax my curls with chemicals, heat, and any other products that were advertised to make me look more white.

The next schools I'd attended were not majority black, but my peers asked about my ethnicity often. When Mom realized I was catching onto her bluff, she finally told me I was Puerto Rican. Inspired by the MTV show, *Sweet 16*, I started to plan a quinceañera for myself. While googling ideas for the party and "Puerto Rican traditions," I knew I didn't resemble the women on the screen. The more the search engine revealed, the more the mirror revealed to me that I am a white *and* black woman.

The last time Mom and I ever talked about race, I asked her why she didn't want me to know I was black. Her face fell into her hands and she wept. She told me when she was in school people made fun of the mixed kids, even more than the black kids. I know now my Mom wasn't ashamed of my race. Instead, she was trying to do everything she could to protect me from the aggression I wouldn't come to notice until later in my life.

But because Mom didn't make a big deal about my race growing up, neither did I. It never felt like the most important part of my identity.

Many of my cohorts identify themselves as "transracial adoptees." I rarely do—not because I believe in color blindness but because members of the black community have done to me what my Mom did. They tell me I am not black. This has caused much turmoil, frustration, and confusion in me.

Time and time again, I have been verbally attacked and bullied online because I am light-skinned, because I married a "privileged" white man instead of a black man, because I express pro-life beliefs, and because I want to support law enforcement who protect and even save abused children.

When I say I am black, black people tell me I have a lot to learn and I need to listen up; but I have rarely been asked about my experience as a black person from a black person, no matter how much I listen.

It is evident when you look at me, I am not just Caucasian but mixed. In American culture, the "one drop rule" says I am black, but to many black people, I am white.

And the experience cuts both ways. To so many white people in my life, although my skin held next to theirs can be a similar shade (or sometimes an even lighter shade) and even though my mother's blood weaves itself into my story just as deeply as either one of their parents, I am black. I've experienced other moments of marginalization from white folks beyond just skin color conversations. For instance, I love my black culture. Getting my hair braided and a full set of nails makes my heart full. The music and dancing that erupt from the black community make me feel elated. And sadly, I've experienced cutting words when advocating for these elements of my black culture. Or, in another example, I'll never forget when I wanted to speak with a white family member about racial reconciliation, and they told me they didn't wish to speak about *that* because God tells us in Scripture to seek what is *good*, and *that* didn't seem like a good topic to talk about.

God knitted in each of us a desire to belong. To belong with His church, His creation, His people, ultimately because we desire to be with Him. In foster care the desire felt amplified. In each home, with each family, I shape-shifted myself to be like them with hopes to be accepted by them. Just as foster care couldn't find a home for me, our society hasn't found a place for me either.

I don't feel like I belong squarely in the BIPOC (black/indigenous/people of color) community because they say my light skin grants me too much privilege and I hold views too conservative. I don't feel like I belong among conservatives because my social justice drum beats too loud. I don't feel like I belong among political progressives because I refuse handouts without showing vulnerable populations how *they* can hand out. Nor do I belong among theological progressives because I believe Jesus Christ is actually God and He actually rose from the dead after bearing our actual sins on the cross. I don't feel like I belong among former and current vulnerable populations because I appear privileged now. I don't feel like I belong among the privileged because I can tell by the way they shift in their seats that my talking about my background makes them uncomfortable. But at the same time, I don't really mind not belonging. I find comfort in my identity being a daughter of the King.

I could choose to have hurt feelings about not belonging (and sometimes I have), but instead I choose to stand firm in knowing where I've come from, who God has made me to be, and where He is sending me. My identity is BIPOC *and* Caucasian whether those communities want to claim me or not. I like my conservative convictions, and I will also advocate like progressives whether they want to claim me or not because Proverbs 31:8 says, "Speak up for those who cannot speak for themselves." My background is vulnerable and my future is privileged because that is what I am called to. Because that's the story God has written for me thus far, and I dare not take the pen from Him. I like not fitting into any identity society has pigeonholed, politicized, and polarized because my true identity transcends.

~ * * * ~

There is nothing Mom wanted more for me as a little girl than to some-day be an educated woman.

"You have to go to college."

"You can't get pregnant until you have a bachelor's degree."

And she occasionally added, "Having a baby will ruin your life."

When we moved again, this time to Bowling Green, Ohio, she added another precondition, "You can't attend college here," and proceeded to explain to me, at just eight years of age, that the college reported the most STDs among students in the entire nation.

I'd joined Mom and Daddy Isaac at work since I didn't have school for the summer. Their office was a 1996 Chevrolet Astro van referred to as "The Kirby Van." The trunk was filled with boxes of overpriced vacuum cleaners Mom and Issac set out to sell, from morning 'til night.

While Isaac was selling enough Kirbys, Mom was selling a lot. Once Mom sold so many she was given her own office. To say Mom was good at her job would be an understatement.

Mom would hire nearly anyone with aspirations to give them a new start. Daily morning meetings were held at our house. I'd wake up to Mom happily screaming, "Think!" And her vivacious team would shout back, "Positive!"

"Think!"

"Positive!"

"Think!"

"Positive!"

Mom had a knack for making people who others would feel uncom-fortable around comfortable in our home. She wasn't much of a cook, but she was happy to offer people Jimmy Dean microwavables or doughnuts. Picking up strangers off of the streets and letting people live in our home didn't phase me. It was our normal.

The house we lived in was the nicest we'd ever had. The development on Anna Street was new to town. The neighborhood was my favorite I'd ever lived in because many of my friends from school lived close by. We drove around on our electric scooters to meet one another, and a few of us even had trampolines.

Once we could afford for me to stay home, Mom hired nannies. A batch of them came and went, and I rarely saw Mom. But at nighttime when she arrived home, if I wasn't asleep, she was sure to make time for me.

Mom and I sat on the couch with two forks eating the brownies straight from the pan. I cuddled my head into her chest. On the television, we watched a show where a skinny, black man with gold teeth and a clock necklace licked faces with multiple girls on the same day. All of the girls lived in the same house and fought often. The most memorable fight was when Pumpkin spit in New York's face.

By the end of the night, the man offered each woman her own over-sized clock necklace, unless he was not interested in continuing the relationship with her. The women who didn't receive a clock had to go home. They'd walk out of the house throwing their middle fingers in the air screaming bleeped-out cuss words while Mom and I just cackled at the television.

~ * * * ~

By nine years old, I was practiced at dealing with emergencies and familiar with hospitals. Mom had several allergic reactions to soybean oil, a few mental breakdowns, and at least one suicide attempt that she had to be hospitalized for.

When Mom had spent time in jail, I looked forward to visits with her, but visiting Mom in coping centers and mental hospitals was something I dreaded every time. The doctors often detoxed her from prescribed medication and her drugs of choice. Locked in, on the opposite side of the door, Mom would scream that she needed her medication, the loudest I've ever heard her scream. It was as if Mom were possessed, as she repeatedly slammed herself into the door and walls. I felt scared but never for myself. For her. I knew I was safe because of the secure facility with heavy doors and big, electronic, metal locks. But from what I understood about Mom's mental illness, I didn't feel she was safe.

The medication calmed her brain and relieved pain from her body. I can't know what goes on in Mom's brain, but with the trauma she'd experienced and the chemical imbalances she'd been professionally diagnosed with, I could imagine her brain was a scary place to pitch a tent. When Mom was off her meds, she had to live in the brick house between her ears. Without her medication, there were no huffing-and-puffing breathing techniques able to blow the trauma away.

If Mom came out of her room at the coping center, she was dazed. We sat across a table from each other, with nurses standing by to supervise as Mom slid a jewelry box over to me. A foam cartoon ballerina, performing a pirouette, was glued to the top.

"I made this for you, sweetie." Hospitals were places where people went to get better and I didn't doubt that Mom went to the hospital to get better for me because, as she always said, everything she did was for me. I could believe that Mom did everything for me to attempt to heal my own wounds. But the reality is, *everything* wasn't for me, but as a mom now, I see much of what she sacrificed was for me.

~ * * * ~

The men and women who worked for Mom weren't your typical clean-cut, businesspeople. Most of them had tattoos and piercings. The men sagged the crotches of their pants mid-thigh or lower. The women usually wore skirts too tight and shirts that revealed their cleavage.

Mom was different. She knew how to dress so that people with money would respect her and allow her into their homes; and even more so, Mom knew how to thrift. She'd spend hours in thrift shops showing me what was good quality or, at least, what could pass as good quality.

I'd quickly get bored in Goodwill, but Mom's coworkers accepted her help. They'd patiently pick through each aisle together. I think she was so good at having patience for people who had little because she spent time in their position.

Mom wanted me to have a better life than the one her parents gave her, and I believe she wanted that for everyone else as well. So when her employees left the thrift shop with an entirely new wardrobe and a better idea of how to dress like a professional, Mom would generously pay.

Those working for Mom were searching for a new beginning. And even though many would have said she wasn't mentally stable enough to do so, Mom maintained the Kirby business, I think, because she genuinely wanted to offer people an opportunity to have a good life.

~ * * * ~

When Mom and Isaac married, Isaac had two children from two other women. But throughout four years of marriage, two other kids had come to Isaac declaring him as their father. The DNA tests confirmed the truth, which made Mom responsible for child support.

Isaac swore he'd never have another kid, but when Mom got pregnant again, she swore she'd never have another abortion. So Isaac threatened to leave and disappeared for long periods of time. The cycle of waiting for Isaac's return seemed endless. But when he returned, Mom welcomed him as if he never left.

During a cold, grey morning, Mom drove me to the bus stop even though I usually walked. My wet shoe prints stamped upon the gray van carpet that matched the sky in color. I shivered in the back seat, grabbing the zipper on my coat, when Mom suddenly spun around from the front seat to hand me an electronic device with velcro on one side and buttons on the other. "Place this on the bottom of the seat."

"What is it?" I asked as I stuck it below where I sat.

"A recorder."

The bus pulled up. "Make sure you push the red button," Mom said before murmuring something about "catching that son of a . . . cheating . . . lying . . ." She shook her head back and forth and stared out at the windshield.

I returned home that evening to no Isaac and a manic mom. She walked around the house cleaning frantically while talking on the phone—proudly and happily telling friends, family, and coworkers that the recorder worked. She "caught him" and "nothing could get past her."

After my bath, I strutted to Mom in a similar way she had been strutting for hours. "You promise you won't be mad?" I asked.

"Did you spill nail polish on the carpet?"

"No."

"What'd you do?"

I stuck my nine-year-old leg out. "I shaved my legs."

She laughed and hopped on the phone again with friends and family members just to tell them her baby girl shaved for the first time. Soon after she'd spent some time on the phone, she marched toward me. Her eyes were worried. Her mania was not simmering down anytime soon. If anything, it was ramping up.

"Do not use Brandy's razor," she demanded. "If you do, you will get an STD." Brandy was another one of Mom's coworkers whom Mom had offered a place to live so she could get her feet back underneath her. Mom sprinted up the plush, white-carpeted steps, directing me to follow behind her. She pulled the cleaning products out from underneath the sink and dropped to her knees to teach me how to thoroughly scrub the bathtub Brandy and I shared.

~ * * * ~

Mom screamed from the kitchen and Brandy wept. I stayed upstairs, slowly and quietly pulling my dresser drawers out to get ready for school. Grabbing my shoes, but not daring to put them on so my steps made the least amount of noise as possible, I tiptoed down each stair, with my eyes on the door, trying to avoid bringing any attention to myself.

But Mom already had a plan for the day in mind. Instead of going to my third-grade classroom, I was accompanying them on a field trip to an abortion clinic.

Mom never explained to me what an abortion was, but she talked to me as if I knew. "You need to know how hard this decision is. This is what happens if you get pregnant, Victoria, so don't go sleeping around," Mom told me while the three of us drove in the car. Brandy continued to stay silent. "This is a very hard thing to do, but this is real life. This is why you don't get pregnant."

People stood outside of the gray building with signs and large crosses, but Mom and Brandy kept their eyes from meeting theirs.

As we sat in the cold waiting room with gray carpet, plaster walls, and cheap metal chairs, Mom held Brandy's hand and I held Mom's. A lady eventually called Brandy back to some procedure room, and Mom and I went outside to wait in the car.

After some time, Mom pulled to the back of the building where Brandy stood alone as she clutched a plastic bag. Mom opened the door as Brandy moved slowly toward the car. Gripping the top of the vehicle door, Brandy slipped onto the seat. On the way home, her sobs were loud enough for me to know that whatever an abortion was, I didn't want one.

Chapter 4

ABUSED

There are three beatings I distinctly remember. The first, I was in the fourth grade.

Mom's moods were the worst in the mornings because she had yet to take her medication. I don't recall why Mom was angry, but she woke up early enough to catch me before I left for school. My strategic ways of getting ready without being seen or heard usually kept the beast asleep, but on this particular morning she caught me just as I went to leave.

The back of my oversized shirt wadded, leaving my low back exposed to the burn of the carpet as Mom dragged me through the house. Mom climbed on top of me and pinned my legs closed with hers so I couldn't kick. As she hit me, she told me I ruined her life, called me a "product of rape," and "a spitting image of a rapist." I remember this beating because it was the first time she used words like that, and even though she was beating me, it wasn't until she said those words that I started to cry.

She opened and closed her fists against my body as I tried to catch my breath. Suddenly, she fell to the floor in what appeared to be agony. She cried and covered her face as if she expected me to hit her the same way she hit me.

After, it became more common for Mom to call me a "product of rape," and "a spitting image of a rapist." A box that had never been opened before now allowed for words to come out like wild snakes, biting and too savage ever to be captured again. As I became older, I understood that something about me triggered Mom. I didn't have to do anything to set her off because I was a reflection and a reminder of the people who hurt her most.

Since Mom was a prostitute, and even jailed for solicitation of prostitution, of course I've wondered if I was actually the outcome of a trick. I could never truly know—not because I don't think people should believe abuse victims who disclose rape (they should) but because of the way her particular mental illness intersected with my age and abilities to understand things as a nine-year-old. In her mind, from what I could tell, pieces of the story rattled around in a whirlwind, flew out of her mouth out of order at random times, and then came to lodge themselves within my young brain in a jumbled way. In these ways, back then, it was hard to know what actually happened. However, I am convinced she was telling the truth when I look back and see how disturbed she was by my presence at times, even when she tried so hard to love me well.

While Mom hugged herself in a fetal position, I took the opportunity to run. The bus was just pulling up. When I sat in my assigned seat on the bus, next to the same girl I sat next to every day, I lifted up my shirt to expose the bruises on my hips and ribs. Her eyes grew large, and then her face winced when she saw the black-and-blue marks.

I remember because I didn't know what to say. I stayed silent, but I was hoping she would say something. I hoped she would know what to say. I remember because I thought she would ask me where the bruises came from so I didn't have to hold onto the secret any longer. I remember because I hoped she would tell someone else who could help me. I remember because no matter how much I wished someone would, she didn't say anything about the bruises or ask about the pain, and neither did anyone else.

~ * * * ~

Since Mom decided to give birth instead of abort, Isaac's presence became unpredictable. Mom explained to me that we were named after queens because we should be treated like queens, but I doubted if a queen would tolerate a so-called king who left and came back whenever he pleased.

The hospital room was dark, and Mom's moaning and groaning felt like it went on for hours. I eventually fell asleep and woke when the nurse tapped me. We walked down a long hallway to the room that contained what I'd been hoping to gain for almost ten years—a sister.

The nurse slowly closed the door, as I tiptoed toward the baby bed. My baby sister, Allison, slept peacefully, her entire body wrapped in a white blanket with colored baby foot prints on it. I felt like if I took my eyes off of her I'd be missing something, but the only movement was the rise and fall of her dainty chest. I slowly brought my hand to hers, which brought a wave through my stomach. Her frailty was overwhelming, but I couldn't stop the urge to pick her up.

I looked at the tile floor, terrified of what would happen if I tripped. My eyes followed my feet, so I knew exactly where to step. And somehow at the same time, my eyes never left Allison. I sat down in the chair next to Mom and held my sister against my chest. I observed her cheeks, button nose, and long eyelashes, and cried. She was the best thing I'd ever known.

~ * * * ~

Soon after giving birth, Mom got in a car accident that injured her back. Isaac was coming and going until he was gone for good. Nannies suddenly became unaffordable, and Mom decided I was old enough and responsible enough to take care of Allison.

Vacuum boxes were perfect for moving, so Mom picked up the business and waved her hand for me to follow along.

Defiance, Ohio, wasn't too far from where we lived. There were rows of mobile homes right in the middle of one of the busiest parts of town, directly across from the mall. The moving truck hurled each time we hit a pothole in the trailer park. Mom parked in front of a brown-and-white trailer, at the end of a row closest to the mall, where a woman leaned on a rusted car outside.

"How many cats did you have?" Mom asked.

The woman's responses were too soft for me to hear, but Mom was nearly screaming.

"It'll take a lot for us to clean that out, and I'm sure there are plenty of cats under the trailer too."

The door was falling off of the hinges, and a few of the windows were broken.

"We have to replace nearly everything. It'll cost us a fortune. I'll give you $600 for it."

The cat lady nodded her head. Mom knew how to make a deal. I unbuckled Allison, put her on my hip, and followed Mom inside the trailer. As soon as the door opened, the odor of cat urine stunned me. I held my breath as I observed the written cuss words, pictures of drawn demons and genitalia, and spray-painted graffiti on the walls.

"Are we going to live here?" I asked Mom.

"Yes!" Mom exclaimed. "But it's not going to look like this when we're done with it."

Though I don't remember saying it, Mom said my response was: "You could have gotten us a better place than this."

This statement still lives with me. Mom continues to tell me how ungrateful I was growing up because of those ten words. These words struck a chord with Mom. They hurt her feelings because she really was giving her best. And that's just it: Mom was always doing her best to fight the trauma, to combat the mental illness, to raise us girls better than she was raised.

That night we slept on the floor of the living room with a space heater next to all three of us. We all cuddled under one blanket. I struggled to sleep because Allison cried more than normal, and the smells overbore me. Some nights, when all fell silent, Mom left in the middle of the night to come back before morning. We slept like this for some time until one morning, Mom's man-friends showed up to help us.

We ripped out walls, nailed up new drywall, tore up the floor, laid a new carpet, painted walls, and put in a brand-new shower. Mom did a lot of work herself with the guidance of some guys who were more acquainted with remodeling.

When the remodeling was finished, we drove to a storage unit and filled our house with Mom's belongings. Mom's wrap-around couch, dark oak wardrobe, antique vanity, and big-screen television didn't seem to fit in the trailer. Regardless, Mom had a style that was almost royal. She even hung an original Thomas Kinkade painting on the wall in our hallway that previously had a large cuss word written out in permanent marker. Eventually, the house became so filled that Mom started joking about how we had to do "the wiggle" to get to where we were going.

We'd move our hips back and forth a little more than necessary and look at one another laughing when trying to get from the kitchen to the toilet.

~ * * * ~

The owner of the trailer park was April's father, which made April like the princess of the trailer park. Mom had a knack for making friends with people who had influence, and she and April became the best of friends quickly. April was around Mom's age and lived about two hundred meters diagonally from us, so we spent a lot of time at her house.

I loved April. She told me I could walk into her house anytime. She fed me sweet foods Mom would have never bought and let me play video games Mom would never let me play.

One night, Mom, April, and Heath (April's boyfriend) went out to Spanky's, the local bar in town. Mom was staunch about never drinking and driving, so I imagine she walked home before I heard her stumbling over her words and her feet. Mom was always loud, but this particular night she was even louder.

I quickly shutdown MySpace, blackened the computer screen, rushed to my and Allison's room, and jumped under the covers to act as if I were sleeping.

I didn't know who Mom was talking to, but she kept saying that April and Heath weren't married and April needed to "get a grip" if she thought she "owned a man who clearly didn't want to put a ring on it." It became clear to me through Mom's monologue what Mom and

Heath did, and though April and Heath had been together for years, Mom felt little to no remorse.

When the trailer park and Mom finally fell silent, I fell asleep. But just a few hours later, I was jolted awake by Mom and April screaming at each other outside. I peeked outside to realize that though Mom fell silent, she hadn't fallen asleep. Every parent that walked their kid to the bus stop glared over the chalk-written letter Mom had scribed in enormous letters on the driving path directly in front of our trailer. Some even stood over it, taking pictures and videos. Mom's handwriting was neat, and each word exposed April in only the way a best friend could.

April and Mom pointed at each other, screaming and calling each other names. Neither of them seemed to care that they had an audience of startled children and tired parents. Still in my pajamas, I rushed to the kitchen to find the largest pot and fill it with water. I couldn't carry it when filled to the brim, so I dumped half of it and ran outside as fast as my twelve-year-old legs could carry me, splashing the water onto my garments, trying my best to keep as much water in the pot as possible. Once I got to the chalk-written letters, I dissolved the words piece by piece, one half-pot of water at a time.

Embarrassed for Mom and sad for April, I knew that the friendship was lost. A deep responsibility to save the relationship and heal the pain overtook me.

I've always felt responsibility to save Mom in various ways. I don't know if it was founded during this particular instance or if it was embedded into my thoughts each time Mom told me I saved her life when she found out she was pregnant with me.

Either way, the savior complex has been a hard one for me to shake, especially when it comes to Mom. It is freeing to know that I don't have to be the Messiah because, as I eventually found out years after the chalk-letter incident, Christ already is. But it is also a fine line to figure out as a believer.

As I've said before, Mom and I are similar, but I believe the greatest difference between us is that I have the church, and she doesn't.

Her community is futile. Mine is steadfast. Her community is self-serving. Mine is others focused. Her community tells her to love herself. My community helps me understand the unchanging love God has for me. It makes a big difference. Truly, I credit the body of Christ, the church, for where I am today. A bunch of Jesus-loving people who were compelled to love me because of His love for them. Because He first loved.

Understanding God loves me compels me to influence others to know Him, so they can know how loved they are by Him. And I know well that people are rarely influenced by what we say. Rather people are compelled and moved by who we *are*. So we must be the hands and feet of Jesus, not just the mouths.

When taking care of the widow and orphan, saving seems natural. It is well intended, but it's a responsibility we cannot bear because we were never meant to. We are called to love, not save.

Chapter 5

VIOLATED

Mom's new boyfriend Berry was a tall, handsome fella with a southern drawl similar to Mom's. I don't remember much about him, other than that I wasn't a fan of his, because he'd yell at Mom for being "sleazy" and scream at her for having two kids from different men. When I asked Mom why she kept him around, she said I needed a male model and father figure in my life, which didn't make much sense to me because I had Uncle Allen, Mom's brother and only sibling.

I spent the night at Uncle Allen's house often. He worked hard and showed me how to build and fix all types of contraptions. He'd take me out to eat and let me play on his computer for hours.

Occasionally, he'd show me naked women on his computer or phone, but every time he apologized and said it was an accident. Growing up, the men in Mom's life had a plethora of pictures and videos around the house that resembled what Uncle Allen showed me; and when I told Mom I found those, she usually laughed and told me not to go looking (though I didn't have to), so I dismissed what Allen showed me.

Uncle Allen lived by himself since he was divorced but spent a lot of time at his friend's house. His friend's wife was Mandy, and she had three kids—two sons and one daughter. Mom claimed out loud and shamelessly to anyone that the daughter wasn't Mandy's husband's but my uncle's. My suspicion grew when Uncle Allen would sleep in the same bed as Mandy and her husband when we stayed at Mandy's house.

For my seventh-grade social studies class, I had to make a brochure on the computer and print it out, and since Mom didn't have a printer, I went to Uncle Allen's to use his. After I completed the assignment, it was late, and he told me if I spent the night, he'd drive me to school the next morning.

Uncle Allen expressed he was so impressed by my brochure that he wanted me to make one for his business and asked me to show him what program I used. As I proudly navigated him through the different ways to create a pamphlet, he placed his hand on top of mine to guide the mouse to his photo files. He said sorry when pictures of exposed women popped onto the computer screen and then clicked on the different images he wanted to put in the brochure.

I crawled into bed and fell asleep. Uncle Allen crawled in with me, which woke me up. I lay there acting as if I were asleep, afraid something worse might happen if I showed him I was actually awake. I imagined saying or doing something, but then I imagined making the scenario worse. Uncle Allen moaned and moved. I stayed immobile.

I thought it would all stop, but it didn't, so I shot out of bed.

"I think I will sleep better at home." I said calmly.

He looked shocked, "What do you mean? I can't drive you home now. It's too late."

I started to walk toward the door. "If you don't drive me home, I'll walk home." Uncle Allen lived miles from the trailer in the country. If I started walking, I wouldn't have even known which way to go.

"Why? Why do you want to go home?"

I quickly came up with a lie I thought would be convincing. "I remembered I have to ride the bus tomorrow to help my friend with her homework."

Uncle Allen attempted to negotiate. "I can drive you to the bus stop instead of to school."

"We will have to wake up too early for that."

Uncle Allen looked scared. I felt powerless. He negotiated with me again, "You can go home, but you have to take a shower first."

I felt gross anyway. I shut the door to the bathroom and quickly showered. When I was dressed, I stood by the front door. Uncle Allen sat on the couch, his eyes pointed toward the floor, his shoulders slouched forward and down. "You don't love me anymore?" He asked sadly.

This man had saved me from countless manic episodes from Mom. He was my refuge. I couldn't rationalize not loving him, but I hated the way he made me feel that night. I justified his actions by assuming he forgot he was at his house and thought he fell asleep with Mandy, like usual. He was probably dreaming.

There are many things I didn't understand then that I do now. Me taking a shower was a better deal for him than me staying the rest of the night. I'd be clean of his evidence and no one would believe a poor, young, trailer-park girl who grew up with a mentally ill mother and probably had a mental illness herself. I also now know my uncle was grooming me. He filled my need for a manly hero, saved me from Mom's outbursts, took me out to nice restaurants, and gained my trust because it all led to an easy avenue to abuse me.

"I didn't say that. I didn't say I didn't love you. I'd never say that." I replied. "I just think it is best for me to go home."

At home I fell asleep in my winter coat. The morning doom and gloom doubled down when I realized I didn't wake up to catch the school bus. When I asked Mom to drive me to school, she called me lazy and told me I'd never amount to anything if I didn't value education enough to wake up early and get on the bus.

She continued her lecture in the car about how I needed to attend college unless I wanted to be homeless or sell myself for money. I screamed, begging her to stop, but she only got louder. The car veered toward the other lane. I sat in the front seat, curled into a ball, trying to defend myself from Mom's blows or another car. Mom quickly straightened the wheel and said we were driving to the police station to tell the cops I tried to kill her on the road.

I was relieved when we finally pulled up to the school building. I rushed out of the car and ran to the doors, feeling safe inside the institution of public education. At my locker, I organized and gathered my belongings for class only to notice that the brochure assignment wasn't in my bag.

I stood alone in the hallway, but Mom screamed in my head. The hallway was empty, but it felt narrow as if the walls were crushing me. I started to panic, unable to catch my breath, and fell to the floor. Afraid someone might walk out of class and witness my breakdown, I ran to the restroom to lock myself in a stall. I started hitting myself and calling myself names and declaring Mom right. If I couldn't even catch the bus or hand in a brochure when it was due, how would I ever amount to anything?

~ * * * ~

I've done EMDR (Eye Movement Desensitization and Reprocessing), and I've taken enough psychological medication to know I can't handle yelling, harsh tones, and insults all at once. For so long I thought I could become strong enough to handle it. If I just prayed more, trusted God more, and grew my faith, God would take the triggers away. And that's even what I heard from voices in the church. It's been about twelve years since I've lived with Mom and eight years since I've come to know Jesus, and though I know He can heal me of my trauma, He hasn't done so fully.

I don't like having triggers or trauma. My life would be easier if I didn't, but I do. So I choose to change my perspective and see trauma as an invitation. On the flip side of every trigger is an invitation from God to heal from the damage. Triggers and suffering are painful, sometimes excruciating, but things God can turn for good as He uses them to get our attention, reveal what needs to be healed, remind us to draw near to Him—to remember the Truth that I am loved as I am, not for what I do.

For those Christians with mental illness, we know drawing near to God is the answer, but it is difficult to do. My anxiety would tell me I didn't have enough time to slow down and be. And even if I were to just *be*, it wouldn't be enough for God. If I were to rest, even my rest would not be good rest. God would never say, "Well done my good and faithful servant," when I arrived in heaven. These thoughts easily entangle me.

The idea of God's not saying, "Well done my good and faithful servant" felt like a loophole I found in God. Like if He died for me and I couldn't do anything more to be more loved by Him, then why would He ever say, "Well done"?

As a little girl, I craved for Mom to tell me that I was enough as I am. Today, I crave for God to tell me the same thing.

I didn't come to the realization that I was projecting Mom's character and my trauma onto God until I accepted anti-anxiety medication. The church is starting to learn about these things. Thankfully, our language is changing around issues of mental illness. But for a long time I thought if I went on medication, I wasn't trusting God to heal me or believing in the power of God to heal me. My faith has been everything to me since I've met Jesus. It's where I've found myself and every beautiful gift from God, but I thought if I took medication, then I wouldn't have an adequate faith. For so long I also believed if I went on medication, that meant I'd lost the power of my mind. And if I'd lost my mind, maybe I'd lose my Faith, which is scary because I know it is my Faith that has allowed me to persevere.

In 2020, I finally accepted that my mind is fleshly—meaning, it is fallen. It needs help to move back toward health and wholeness just like any other fallen part of our existence as humans. Our hearts and souls and physical bodies are fallen and fleshly and in need of rescue, regeneration, restoration, resurrection. And, if we think about it, it's clear we trust God to minister to those needs in both miraculous and ordinary ways. For example, if an aging person breaks a brittle bone, she prays for healing from God. She might even enlist her prayer-warrior friends to intercede similarly. And sometimes God answers that request by miraculously healing the bone Himself in the blink of an eye, while other times He answers through a doctor at the local hospital who wraps the bone in a cast and gives it the biological space it needs to mend slowly. Both of those situations point to the truth that the human body is weak and fallen, and both of those situations are evidences of God's hand of healing. His immediate intervention as the Great

Physician is a gift to the world, and so are the medical professionals He chooses to use as instruments of His wisdom and help and healing.

And so, as I said before, 2020 was the year I realized that my mind was just as fallen as a brittle bone that needs a cast or a heart condition that needs blood pressure medication. The health of my mind was just as important as the health of any other part of human beings—and if God was not choosing to miraculously heal me in the blink of an eye, it did not mean He didn't want to heal me at all. Maybe He was going the route we call ordinary. That just felt like such a rarity in my life. Since knowing Christ, I'd witnessed Him as the Love Man of Miracles. But He is also one of steadfast, slow faithfulness. And so, after seeing someone about the trauma I had endured and the ways it was affecting my mind, I accepted my first official psychological diagnosis of Complex Post Traumatic Stress Disorder and started to take prescription medication. I've never felt more healthy and safe inside my brain.

As for faith, I didn't lose it. After all, faith is a spiritual gift from God. As long as I desire faith, He freely gives it.

As for triggers, when someone is harsh toward me I either fight, fly, or fawn. I yell back, leave, or my most popular response, historically at least, is to fawn.

The fawn response is another reaction to trauma that involves immediately trying to please people to avoid conflict. This is often a response developed in childhood trauma, where a parent is the abuser. Children attempt to be pleasers to avoid abuse.

When we see drug abuse, mental illness, screaming, withdrawing, and violence, we can identify that these behaviors often stem from trauma. But what we don't realize is that perfection can be a sign of trauma too. This can look like pleasing everyone around you, being attuned to others' emotions and needs—even hypervigilant to read the room—and struggling to become aware enough of one's own needs. What is a perfect, performing, successful child who does not know her own emotions? An adult with a mental illness so hidden, everyone is shocked when she finally breaks down. Healthy adults and children are not only able to identify others' needs, but they are able to identify their own.

We all want our children to be people who care for others, but what we should want is children ready and willing to confront their mistakes and downfalls without those mistakes shamefully crushing them. A healthy child does not simply communicate and meet others' needs. A healthy child constantly communicates and adapts to meet her own needs without feeling like a burden to others.

~ * * * ~

Al started coming around as Mom's new boyfriend, and Uncle Allen started to come around more than ever, especially when Mom wasn't home.

I couldn't look at him; my body wouldn't let me. Whenever he entered the room, my shoulders and eyes all seemed to aim in the same direction, unmoving. He came back again and again and even offered to fix the electrical issues with the trailer Mom had been begging him to fix for some time. I heard them argue about prices often, and Allen knew we couldn't afford the prices he charged; but guilt might have been the reason he finally offered to fix the issues for free.

Anxiety engulfs me the same way it did my mother.

"You have to go to college, or you'll never get a job."

"Never drink and drive. Never get in a car with anyone who has ever had a sip of alcohol."

"If you get pregnant, your life will be ruined. Do not have a baby before you go to college."

"Check to see if she's breathing," she'd tell me as she gestured toward my sister, the same way I tell my husband, "Check to see if they are breathing," as I refer to my sleeping children.

"Put him inside so I don't run him over," I tell my husband as I gesture toward our toddler before driving away.

"Make sure the oven isn't on. The house could burn down while we are gone," I say even though no one has cooked a meal today.

"We don't have enough money," I declare as I imagine myself and my children homeless and without food because my husband bought a piece of thrifted furniture for 5 percent of the original price.

Mom wrapped up anxiety like it was a present to keep me safe. Unwrapping it was second nature, but when I opened the box, it exploded on me like glue mixed with glitter. It's been on me my whole life, and I'm still trying to scrub it off.

When Uncle Allen offered to fix the electricity, I felt it on me. I silently hoped Mom would deny the offer, but she never rejected anything that was free, which was partially why our trailer looked like an antique dollhouse.

"Well things seem to be working pretty well now!" Mom exclaimed proudly.

I shot my eyes toward her to see if she was being manic or serious.

~ * * * ~

Not going to Uncle Allen's house meant spending more time with Mom. Her outbursts seemed to become more frequent, but I had fewer places to hide. I cannot help but relate this time of my life to how the COVID-19 pandemic isolated the most vulnerable children.

When Mom sold Kirbys, I didn't see her often. Less contact meant less reasons for a quarrel. Naturally. But as I've aged, I think her mental illness needed a place to manifest, and work was a healthy place for mania. But when she was at home for too long, her mental illness manifested into my abuse.

I think stay-at-home moms rock. I'd go so far as to say that kiddos need at least one parent at home, but I also think we all have a little mental weakness in us to some degree, and working as a mom has allowed my mind to have an outlet. While some say work is a distraction from "real feelings," I believe work is a place where I have been able to find the purpose and plan God has for my life. The work that God has gifted me He has used to heal me. After not being heard in foster care, I am now given the microphone. I have learned forgiveness when I train the same people who caused so much hurt in me. I have witnessed the strength of the Holy Spirit as I am granted the energy to continue running the race He has set out for me. I don't know what narrative my children will tell, but I believe I am a better mom because of this work. I think Mom felt that way too.

My weekday escape from Mom was school and the weekend escape was the Skylark, a dance hall for junior high students. I was twelve or thirteen years old now, and my crush was Frankie, a boy who regularly came to the Skylark, chaperoned by his mom. Soon after we met, I started attending church with him because Frankie's mom said we couldn't date unless I did.

Sometimes they'd pick me up and sometimes I'd walk. Though Mom rarely drove me herself, and made clear she didn't want to step into a church, she allowed me to go more often than not. Mom was never against religion. I actually think she was very much for it, and she'd even identify as a Christian herself, being raised in the faith.

Mom could recite Scripture better than many preachers. She most commonly recited Genesis 1:29: "Then God said, "I give you every seed-bearing plant on the face of the whole earth and every tree that has fruit with seed in it," when trying to convince others that marijuana should not be illegal. One time she even said that she prayed God would give her an opportunity to make money and be a stay-at-home mom. "God answered my prayers by giving me drugs. That's why we gotta be careful about what we pray for."

When I went to the church, I was surprised by the loud music and concerned by the guy with long hair and a T-shirt that read "Jesus Freak." He head-banged in the front row even when the music wasn't intense enough to head bang. The pastors came off cool but also weird because they were *maybe* ten years older than me and encouraged us to scream louder if we were having a good time.

The music played around me, and everyone else would sing, but singing made me feel uncomfortable. I usually just watched, impatiently wanting the standing part to end so I could sit down and hold Frankie's hand. One time the pastor asked the crowd if we wanted to worship Jesus with just one more song. I looked him right in the eyes while he stood on stage, and screamed, "No! We just want to sit down!"

Everyone fell silent, and the pastor gloomingly said, "Okay, why don't we all just go to our seats."

This is God's kind of humor, since praise and worship is my favorite part of church now.

My prepaid phone buzzed when worship was *finally* over.

A text came across the screen from my mom threatening to make me live with my uncle. I stepped out of the service unsure of why Mom would say this but sure I could not let it happen. I asked her what happened, and a call came in from her immediately.

I didn't answer when Mom called because I didn't want to tell her the truth, and I knew she'd either ask questions that overwhelmed me or scream at me for not telling her sooner.

Rain poured down as I walked home as slow as I could for three miles. Mom swung the door open and accused me of stealing money from her credit card to put minutes on my phone. Once I reminded her that she had put minutes on the phone the night before she quickly changed the subject without apologizing or admitting she was wrong. "Your uncle waited for you at the church to pick you up. What are you doing here?"

"I didn't want to ride with him, Mom."

Mom stood in my doorway as she came to realize what happened. "That's why you wouldn't go get ice cream with him." She paused. "That's why he offered to fix the electricity for free."

I lay in bed with the blankets over my face. I gritted my teeth and heard the door open. My uncle walked to my doorway. My entire body stayed under the covers, but I knew he was there from the audible wiggles and steps. "Please go away," I pleaded.

"You are just lying so you don't have to come live with me, huh?"

I started sobbing. "I'm not lying. Just please go away. Please."

The pouring rain and dark night were fitting for the scene. He walked away, tried to persuade Mom I was the liar she accused me to be, and left. Mom walked back toward my room.

Mom's voice got soft again. "You know, honey. I don't doubt he did that to you." Mom went on to explain that when she was little he hurt her too, and I questioned how she could have let me spend so much time with him when she was so protective of me.

She started to pace back and forth. "We will have to report it."

"No Mom. Please." I begged.

She continued on. "And if we see him in public, you'll have to point to him and scream what he did to you."

I almost screamed. "Mom, why in the world would I do that?"

"Because that's how you prevent it from happening to others. You make it known!"

Weeks later Mom forced me into a big yellow house where victims reported crimes. Whoever designed it attempted to make it comfortable with plush couches and colorful decor, but cameras were everywhere, and the women who welcomed us at the door were dressed in stale pantsuits.

Mom and I sat in the waiting room that failed to appear as a living room. Mom whispered that foster care would be worse and added, "You know what to tell them and what not to tell them."

Chapter 6

EXPOSED

In the seventh grade, when track practice was announced, Mom purchased me a pair of size eleven track spikes. I wore a size seven at the time, but Mom said she wanted those shoes to be the only shoes she had to purchase for the rest of the year.

My teammates and I changed from our everyday clothes to our running shorts in an outside locker room. The spikes I happily screwed into the bottom of my shoes clicked on the concrete as I walked from the locker room to the track. I walked in a silent confusion noticing the bottom of my team members' shoes did not click when they stepped.

My track coach said, "I love your spikes, Tori! Do you have any other flat shoes?"

I shook my head, realizing I was wearing the wrong shoes but not understanding why the store clerk at the sports store directed us to the shoes I was wearing when we asked him for "track shoes." My coach caught on and explained to me that I would also need flat running shoes for practice. So on my first day of track practice, I ran in my socks.

A couple of weeks later I arrived late, wearing pajama pants to my first track meet. I genuinely thought the pajama pants were track pants. My first ever individual race, the 100-meter dash, I false started. The second race I competed in was the 4x100 relay. I stood in the wrong lane while receiving the baton.

Learning hard lessons young was a blessing in and outside of track.

~ * * * ~

Mrs. K made me feel special, when in front of the entire class, she said she couldn't believe I won races against her daughter. One morning Mrs. K stepped outside the classroom and peeped her head inside the door. As soon as we locked eyes, she waved her finger requesting I step outside of the door. I participated in her class enough for her not to dislike me, but the way she walked with me made me know whatever she had to say held a heavy consequence.

She stopped abruptly on the stair landing, in front of a large window that looked out onto Main Street.

"What are those scratches on your neck?"

I focused my gaze on the street and avoided contact. "My dog scratched me," I said too quickly. We didn't own a dog.

"Those scratches look a bit bigger than dog scratches. They are spread out, more like fingers." She paused. I looked at her wide eyed in silence. I tried to think of another lie or a breed of a large dog I could blame.

"Did you and your mom get into a fight?"

I was in shock that she would suspect anything. Every time I tried to think of a lie to tell her, I knew nothing seemed more realistic than the truth she already knew. She started to walk down the stairs. "We will have to go make some phone calls."

I didn't move and I was determined not to.

"If we tell anyone, the fights will only get worse." I pleaded, "Please don't do this."

I usually struggled to look adults in the eyes, but I watched Mrs. Keller's eyes sink and her shoulders drop. "Sweetie, you won't have to go home again."

Her soft tone urged me on.

After sitting in the guidance counselor's office for some time, a social services woman came. She lifted my clothes to take images of the scratches. I don't remember how much time lapsed since I'd met the caseworkers, but I believe it was only months since I met them in the yellow building that attempted to appear as a house. The same caseworker who interviewed me about my uncle asked me about my homelife.

"We asked you if there was any physical abuse or neglect in the home. Why did you lie to us?"

"My mom told me not to tell you." I shrugged and looked at the ground.

Administration said my mom circled the school outside. I heard the principal and superintendent talk about placing the school on lockdown, but when the school day came to an end, everyone left—except me. I begged them to let me out so I wouldn't miss track practice, but they didn't want Mom to see me before they found a place for me to go.

After many hours of waiting after school, my track coach came to assure me there wouldn't be consequences for missing practice and directed me to a window on the side of the building where there were no door entrances or exits.

"We think your mom is watching the doors." He said before helping me crawl through the window. My guidance counselor waited for me and then drove me to a cousin's house. Sarah was talking to Mom on the phone when I arrived. "No, Lisa. She is wearing a high shirt." I knew better than to wear a low-cut shirt. I wore a sweater bigger than I would usually wear to school that day with hopes that no one would see the scratches. Nonetheless, Mom would still blame the entire scenario on me.

"Yes. She's wearing long sleeves too." Sarah continued to reassure Mom. "I know you were trying to grab her so you could spank her."

My guidance counselor turned to me. "I think most parents stop spanking their kids by this age." I had no response. Mom referred to every blow I received as "spankings" for as long as I could remember.

~ * * * ~

The women who took me in were Mom's cousins, and they were the only family other than my uncle that I remember growing up with. My mom was supposedly court ordered not to see me, and I felt protected by that.

My cousin, Oona, was my favorite. She lent me a Judy Bloom book to read because it was one of her favorite books, but it quickly became my least favorite. By reading the novel, I came to more fully understand what my uncle did to me. I understood why he made me shower, and I came to the conclusion that the images he showed me on the computer were probably never accidental.

Oona and I spent a good amount of time editing our profiles on our MySpace pages. Proud of the work we put in, we wanted to show the mothers of the house our profiles. Oblivious to what we actually did on the computer when we "played," the mothers were stunned to see our hundreds of "friends" and the countless comments about how beautiful I was below my photos.

"You can't post pictures like this." I didn't see what the big deal was. Mom took pictures like this and used a webcam the same way I did. My "private parts" remained private in the photos, covered up by a piece of paper that said, "I am only human."

Voices raised, "What does this mean? You are only human?"

"I don't know. I saw someone else post a picture just like it. They have lots more friends than me." I tried to defend myself and grabbed the mouse to guide them to the profile I found the picture on originally.

The matriarch of the mothers' face flushed red. She snatched the mouse away from me. "Do you know what will happen if men find these pictures?"

Another mother responded quickly, "What Allen did to you."

"Or worse," another mother piped in. "Men will find you, kidnap you, and kill you."

Tears streamed down my face. I felt shame and was astonished that a stupid picture I took caused such animosity.

Oona piped in and shouted, "I was raped, and no one ever says any-thing about it. Everyone always just talks about what happened to Victoria."

Quickly everyone's words clashed and became yells. I tried my best to visualize anything besides Allen's hands brushing against my waist before reaching for my chest. The yells continued as a fist slammed against my ear. All the noise got louder when my head hit the floor. My eyes were closed, but I managed to grab a fistful of hair. Failing at fighting, hoping someone would defend me.

~ * * * ~

An hour or so had gone by, and Mom picked me up from my cousins'. No questions were asked, and no fuss was given by caseworkers or the courts. Mom will still testify today that whenever my caseworker didn't want to deal with me or had too much to do, all restrictions went out of the window, and they sent Mom.

Caseworkers get into the job because their hearts yearn to serve chil-dren and families. But the truth is, caseworkers don't work for children and families. They work for the state and agencies, which in my opin-ion, creates a conflict of interest for many of them.

The average caseload for a child welfare worker is between twenty-four and thirty-one children. Some social workers even handle up to one hundred children or more. On top of this, child welfare workers are expected to conduct intensive investigations, keep a certain number of foster homes in the area, facilitate regular trauma trainings, drive biological parents to parenting classes and rehabilitation treatment, and place abused, neglected, and abandoned children into their forever families. Can you imagine the pressure?

Caseworkers can't adequately advocate for children and families when their caseloads are massive. They can't adequately conduct proper and unbiased investigations in foster homes when they are incentivized to keep a certain amount of foster homes in the county. They can't recruit the best foster parents when the county supervisor pushes the value of quantity over quality, while pressuring caseworkers to meet quotas. Caseworkers can't properly train foster parents to deal with trauma and heartaches when they haven't been able to deal with their own due to the years of trying their best to love abused kids, while seeing the worst.

Caseworkers being overworked and underdeveloped spiritually, mentally, and emotionally is one of the reasons siblings sometimes get separated. It is why some children continue to be placed into one home after the other. It is why trauma continues to manifest in many vulnerable youth, and it is why we continue to lose the potential of some of the most resilient young people in our nation. Of course there are other roles outside of the caseworker within the larger story of foster care in America, and those roles play an important part in all these situations. But the caseworker. As much as their heart breaks for the kids and the families, my heart breaks for them. If I could change one thing about the foster care system today, I'd make it so they no longer had a conflict of interest because the child welfare system has put them in an impossible situation.

~ * * * ~

The break between Mom and me didn't improve our relationship. If anything, it showed me how much better life might be if I didn't live with her. We continued to quarrel, and to her surprise I started to fight back, verbally and physically.

Though Mom continued to pay for the trailer "in case anything happened" between her and Al, Mom moved us to Al's house, which gave us almost six times the space the trailer had to offer.

I was sleeping when Mom came to my bed in the middle of the night. She laid her hand on my shoulder and gently shook me awake. "Victoria, Victoria, wake up. We're going to get Isaac out of jail."

I strapped Allison into her car seat, not giving a second thought to where we were going, until I woke up to realize we were parked in the back of a detention center. Mom was on the phone with a guard explaining that we were outside with the money to bail Isaac out.

Once she got off of the phone, Mom asked, "Honey, where did you get all of that money under your mattress?"

Approximately $500 sat under my mattress. I'd won $100 at the Skylark during a Halloween costume, and the remaining came from the older woman next door, who paid me for washing her dishes, sweeping her carpet, and doing other chores around her house. I couldn't tell Mom I'd saved it up with hopes to run away once I got to $1,000, so I just told her I didn't know where it came from.

Mom was so elated she didn't even care that there was no explanation for half a grand underneath my mattress. "Well, with that money and money from Al, we have enough to get your dad out of jail!"

I didn't claim Isaac as my dad anymore because I'd come to understand my dad was a black man, whom Mom swore got hit by a train and died before I was born. I believed her for a short time when I was young, but at this point I was sure my father was well and alive, and I hoped someday I'd meet him.

Nonetheless, the sneaky nature of going behind Al's back to free Isaac from shackles and bars felt exhilarating, so I matched Mom's excitement. We sat anxiously waiting for Isaac to appear, and when he finally did, he looked nothing like the handsome young dad and businessman I'd remembered. He was scrawny with an untamed beard. On the car ride back, Mom and Isaac talked like they were on their first date.

~ * * ~

After we got Isaac out of jail, he stayed at the trailer while we continued to live at Al's. Since Mom and Al argued most mornings, I usually ran late to school. As we drove down the gravel driveway, he revved the engine and mumbled hateful slurs under his breath. My shoulders tightened, my jaw clenched, and my feet moved side to side trying to shake out the anxiety angry men stirred up in me.

Al's head shot toward the passenger seat to tell me of my "terrible mom" and my inevitability to follow in her footsteps. The names he hurled at me spiraled in my head along with Mom's demeaning voice and words I tried so hard to forget.

My eyes filled with salt water as my throat began to close.

But Al continued, "What is it like being the spawn of such a [expletive]?"

"You'll grow up and be nothing better than a whore."

I was a broken rearview reflection of Mom, and every time he looked into me, he saw the woman who drained him emotionally and financially. Smashing the mirror felt better than moving it.

My ability to spit venom was better than his. I had learned from the best—Mom. It felt as if I swallowed a rock, and that rock would either plug my voice box, keeping the words in, or the rock would come out and hit Al.

The country roads were empty at this time in the morning because most people had already dropped their children off at school and headed to work. As Al continued to get louder and meaner, I imagined opening the door to roll out onto the side of the road and run, but I was too scared of the potential injury and my inability to outrun a truck. Overwhelmed, with tears running down my face, I knew if I let the secret out, it might shut the words off.

"Mom got Isaac out of jail, and he is living in the trailer."

Al slammed on the brakes. My head slammed into the dashboard and my neck whipped back, flinging my skull back to my seat. I opened my eyes and witnessed sparkles frolicking on the road. The truck's wheels screeched as gravel flew up from underneath the tires. Al headed the opposite direction of my bus stop.

Fear filled me. I looked out the window, unable to predict where we were going. I sat silently, regretting my words.

We pulled into the driveway of his house. Slamming the truck door, after jumping out, he trudged to the door. "Get out of the car." He took his saliva to the back of his throat and launched toward me so his tobacco and saliva spit would meet my cheek. He laughed as I clenched my mouth shut and wiped away the brown flakes with my tears.

He flung the door open to the house. He was yelling at my mom now. "Wake up you crazy [expletive]! Did you use my money to get Isaac out of jail?"

My mom stood up with her eyes wide and hair wild.

She flung her body toward mine. I went from standing to the fetal position in seconds, which granted Al easy access to kick my ribs. After throwing high heels at my head, as if it were a dartboard, it was understood that I was not going to school. Bruises covered me from head to toe. The chance a teacher would see hidden contusions on my body when we already had an open investigation was the reason for my frequent absence from school.

Following the typical routine of all the other men, Al kicked us out of his house.

This was the second of the three beatings I distinctly remember.

I remember because it was the first and only time Mom ever let a man hit me. I remember because it was the most pain I had ever been in as a child. I remember because I didn't go to school for days, and even though we had an open investigation, no one came to check on me. I remember because I lay in bed for what felt like a long time. I remember because I called a radio hotline that claimed to help kids, but during the intake process they wanted my address. I remember because I was too scared to give it and hung up on the phone. I remember because I felt hopeless, yet I prayed. I remember because I begged God to take my life. I remember because He didn't.

Chapter 7

IDENTIFIED

When I was growing up, people asked me what I was mixed with and what my ethnicity was. All. Of. The. Time. I said I didn't know, and then people looked at me curiously, wondering why I didn't know my own ancestry.

While dating my husband in college, he experienced it alongside me, people asking me often what my ethnicity was. I told him I wish I knew. I'd like to stop saying I don't know because it felt awkward. So for our first Christmas, he bought me an Ancestry DNA test.

I never did one before because I didn't expect to find my dad's side of the family. I knew that he didn't grow up wealthy and had struggled with drugs, so having access to an Ancestry DNA test was less likely. I also didn't mind so much not knowing my real ethnicity. I was who I was. Not knowing had been more a part of my identity than knowing had.

When the test results came back, my ethnicity was sprinkled all over Europe and various tribes in Africa. To answer people when they asked what I was mixed with would involve my handing them a comprehensive flowchart. That'd be easier than remembering and verbally listing each one.

On my ancestry results, a woman was pictured. She looked so much like me—the shape and color of her eyes, her neck and face structure. The test suggested that she was my aunt. I searched her name and found obituaries of my grandparents and a woman named Venus. The only thing Mom had ever told me about my dad other than his name was that he had a sister named Venus. I knew this was the side of my family I'd never met.

Obituaries said that Venus had left behind more than ten siblings, which gave me enough names to search on Facebook. I found a couple more aunts and sent them this message:

> *Hello . . . My name is Tori. I do not wish to open a book you are not comfortable opening or talk about anything you do not wish to talk about, but I believe you are my aunt or some part of my family and Joe is my father. I was just really hoping to get to know more about my father's side of the family and I would greatly appreciate any conversation or time you would give me. Thank you so much.*

This message began communication with various family members. I learned about a lot of family division and strife, mental illness struggles, histories, and cultures within the family. After about a year of messaging and occasional calls, one of my aunts invited me to come to my birthplace, Houston, Texas, and visit. In June 2019, at twenty-three years old, I was immensely grateful to meet my biological dad's side of the family.

During my visit my aunt took me through photo albums and memorabilia. I held my dad's obituary in my hands, which informed that he was murdered a month before I was born. In that moment I wasn't crushed that my biological father was dead. Even if he were alive while I was out of the womb, the stories I heard of him made him dead to me growing up. At that moment, I felt relieved that Mom hadn't lied and tried to hide my dad from me when he was alive.

In between the more intimate moments, the family put together fun moments for me. They threw me a party with southern comfort food where I got to meet countless relatives. I'll never forget how funny I thought it was when the family asked me if I didn't eat *that* kind of food, what kind of food I could have possibly eaten, as if there was no other kind of food than fried chicken, collard greens, and corn bread.

When my husband Jacob and I weren't visiting with family, we took time to do what we love most—discover new places in nature and food. We took the needed time to rest and debrief together, which made the whole time more enjoyable.

The visit was not crushing, nor was it emotionally difficult for me because God prepared me well. I rest assured that my identity was not in my biological family but in Christ, and I was already loved by God and many that He had surrounded me with. He didn't need to give me anyone else to love me more. I was comforted by the fact that I could not be any more loved than I already was.

I think I was also able to handle this well because of some wisdom given to me by one of my dearest friends. While attending college, I became close to one of my track teammates, Maddie. We remained close after college and still see each other as sisters. Maddie was one of the only other girls at my college who was black and adopted.

She met parts of her biological family just months before I did, and she seemed to handle it with an admirable emotional intelligence. When I asked her how she was doing and why she thought she was doing so well, she offered me the wisdom I carried into meeting my biological family: "I had no expectations."

Not putting a heavy weight on my family to be something or not expecting anything from them made me genuinely thankful for each moment I was able to have with them. Each time they told me a story, it was enough. Every time they picked up the tab and every time they didn't, it was enough. Every minute we spent together and every minute we had apart, it was enough.

I left with a full heart and a full tummy. I knew that the moments I got with my father's family were something other adoptees hope, wish, and pray for. Their hearts ache over it. I knew this time was not to be taken for granted.

~ * * * ~

It seemed like no matter how much I told Mom I didn't mess around, she told everyone else I did. Before my body could be seen as worth anything, it was deemed worthless, which made it feel like it was from the time I was a preteen and on. There was a point when I no longer saw the point of not being all of the things Mom referred to me as. We all have a desperate yearning to be wanted, and mine revealed itself when I let church boys climb through my window and into my bed.

I listened to my youth pastor talk about purity and the importance of it, so I refused to let boys in my pants, but no one taught me that purity included other things as well.

Rumors spread about me being fast. I quickly learned boys liked "bad girls" for a minute, but they wanted "good girls" for a lifetime. I wanted my reputation to change and for people to stop calling me "trailer tramp," so I begged Mom to let me change schools, which after some time she finally allowed.

The rumors followed me, and even though I was a virgin, I was worthless to boys because in their eyes my body had been used in one way or another by every other boy. The only reason I stayed a virgin as long as I did was because I didn't want anyone saying anything worse.

~ * * * ~

Moving schools didn't change my reputation, but it was still the best decision I could have made because it put me exactly where I was supposed to be, allowing me to hear exactly what I was supposed to hear. God redeemed this time by putting me in the English class of Mr. Rodenberger.

Mr. Rodenberger offered high fives to everyone, but he made me feel especially seen when he'd lay his hands on my shoulders and say cheerfully, "I'm glad you're here, kid." Despite my poor grades and lack of effort, Mr. Rodenberger always put effort into encouraging me.

I think, unlike many teachers, every day he remembered why he became a teacher in the first place. He never compromised who he was for the public school system's regulations and rules. And because of his efforts, I held the idea that in his class I was special.

In his class, we went through the book *The Seven Habits of Highly Effective Teens*. Habit number two in the book suggested "beginning with the end in mind."

Mr. Rodenberger explained it like this: "See, the eighth grade is important because you are preparing for high school. You have to work to get good grades now because next year your grades will really count. The grades you get from here on out will be *permanent* on your transcript. Colleges will see those transcripts, and they will decide if you get scholarships to college. It's hard to go to college without scholarships because college is expensive. And if you don't go to college, many of you might end up *just like your parents*."

I stopped listening as reels of my own life replayed themselves in my head. I saw myself being beaten. I saw Mom and her many boyfriends. I saw how I took care of my sister while my mom did drugs. I saw the times I visited Mom in jail. I saw the times I helped Mom check into the psychiatric wards and coping centers.

And then for the first time, God gave me a glimpse of my future. I imagined my future husband and my children. I imagined no separation, no divorce, and my children knowing and loving their father. I imagined safety and security for my children. I imagined a big house where everyone wanted to eat. I imagined making a home and building a family. And as I sat in that classroom, I made a conscious decision to do everything for them, the family I didn't yet know but would someday have.

My grades had consisted of Cs and Ds at the time, so I had a lot of work to do. I had to ask more questions and use my study hour periods as times to work instead of writing notes to friends. I asked for help from my teachers and built relationships with them.

One of the most important correlations I noticed in high school that continued into college was this: the better the relationship with my teacher or professor, the better my grade was. Strong and healthy relationships lead to victory.

Just a couple of months after Mr. Rodenberger's talk, I sat on the computer to check my grades and saw one B sitting on the screen's line of

As. The young man sitting next to me knew what kind of grades I used to receive. He looked at me and the computer, with a confused look, "What kind of grades do you usually get?"

I replied as confidently as I knew how and shrugged, "I get As."

My teacher's speech wasn't necessarily an epiphany but a catalyst that changed the direction I was headed. Though Mr. Rodenberger never said anything about Jesus, he laid a foundation for me that caused me to seek out more complex things in my education, like religion. My education became my confidence and my hobby. As my grades improved, I was placed in advanced classes, which would bring me to ask philosophical questions that eventually led me to God.

In 2015, the college I applied to had an average acceptance GPA of 3.89 and an average ACT score of 31. My ACT score couldn't speak for me—the anxiety felt excruciating each time I was tested, which I'm sure is the reason I tested below the national average—but my GPA and my character were enough. Aside from Mom continually pushing a higher education, I credit Mr. Rodenberger and his class for my acceptance into Hillsdale College. God always receives the glory, but God used a public school teacher, Mr. Rodenberger, as a vessel to change the habits embedded in me, that would eventually make me God's.

Chapter 8

FOSTERED

Since there were no more boys at church interested in me, I had no other reason to go other than Tonya. Tonya was a frail woman who never intended to be flashy. She was thrifty and spoke softly. Her entire essence was gentle. And she was my favorite.

She held a small group at her house where we would bake cookies, eat meals, and make crafts. I asked her once why we didn't read the Bible there, and she replied, "We don't always have to tell people about Jesus. Sometimes we just have to show people." That went right over my head, and I really wouldn't understand it until I was an adult, but the sentiment explains Tonya and the influence she has had over me precisely.

Around 9:00 a.m., Tonya picked my friend, Cindy, and me up at the trailer to head to the Toledo Zoo. We were about forty minutes into the one-hour drive when Tonya received a call from Mom.

I heard her threats through the phone from the back row of the van, which meant each girl in front of me heard too. I told Mom we were going to the zoo, and she had given me permission, but she told Tonya she had to bring me back home immediately, or else she'd call the cops and report her for kidnapping me. Tonya pulled over the van and tried to reason with Mom, but there was no way Mom heard Tonya as she continued yelling. Tonya apologized profusely, but Mom persisted angrily. The more Tonya appeared poised and helpful, the more outraged Mom became.

After some time, Tonya gave up trying to talk through Mom's spats and started to cry. I put my head in my hands and cried when she surrendered and turned the van around to take me and the other girls she ministered to home.

Still on the phone with Mom, Tonya said, "I'm bringing her home now."

Mom's voice suddenly became significantly quieter and sweeter. "No, that's okay. You guys go have fun at the zoo! What time will you be back?"

Stunned, it felt like time stopped.

We caught our breath, just long enough to spend a day at the zoo and get back. I always asked Tonya to pick me up first and drop me off last, and even when the route didn't make sense she gladly did. With an empty van, Tonya came in to apologize to Mom for any miscommunication and to thank her for letting us continue to go to the zoo.

In the midst of the apology, Mom started to blame me and call me names. The hurling insults seemed to never stop, and each time I heard another I hated myself more and more. As Mom screamed, I sobbed and begged Tonya to let me live with her.

This is the third distinct beating I remember. The entire scene changed quickly from a yelling competition between me and Mom to a wrestling match once Mom pinned me to my bed and started hitting me. Tonya fell to her knees and prayed loudly. I can't remember what she said, but she was begging God for mercy through her tears. Then suddenly, out of nowhere, Mom fell to the ground.

I remember because I thought maybe, just maybe God had the power to protect me. I remember because when Mom tells me now that it was all my fault that I went into the foster care system and makes me feel crazy, Tonya reminds me of this story and others that she witnessed. I remember because when I finally came to faith, I have prayed for the Holy Spirit to minister through me for kids like me, like it did in Tonya. I remember because I witnessed the power of prayer and falling on one's knees in the midst of utter desperation.

~ * * * ~

Life at Mom's became increasingly tense. It was a cycle. I grew more rebellious, and Mom grew more intolerant, which made me more rebellious and her more intolerant.

The tape measure on the table was the closest thing to my hand, and when I chucked it at Mom, it had the effect I wanted it to. She stopped attacking me, but I pinned her on the couch and kept hitting her. I still remember her face. She looked terrified, and she asked desperately, like a child, "What are you doing?" I stood over her feeling immediate shame that I had weapons as hands, at the same time I felt relief when I used them.

After Mom rushed to the phone, the police came to our house. Though the atmosphere had calmed down by the time the officers arrived, I was handcuffed and taken to a juvenile detention center.

After intake, fingerprints, and mug shots, I was handed a one-ounce paper cup filled with green soap to take a shower with. When I said I needed conditioner and a brush to take a shower with, the guards laughed at me and said I'd only receive a comb and green soap from here on out. The soap they offered me was to be used for my body, shampoo, and conditioner.

I wet my 3B hair and tried to brush it out with my fingers, but when it was barely damp, the guards yelled, "Times up!" I tried to brush out as many knots as I could before the moisture left the locks, but after just a few days of this pattern, the back of my hair started to mat.

When Mom came to visit, she berated the guards and called the detention center to inform them that they were neglecting my basic needs and if I did not receive conditioner immediately there would be consequences.

Within hours of Mom's departure, I was the first and only girl in the detention center who was able to have a paddle brush and high-quality conditioner. My showers were extended so I had time to brush out my hair, and even though guards told me not to share the conditioner with other girls, I did anyway.

Our paper cups of green soap were set out on a table in front of the shower, so when the guards weren't looking, I put a dollop of conditioner in all of the girls cups. Part of me thinks the guards left them there and didn't look on purpose, knowing I would put conditioner in the cups because there is no other time, other than when we were all locked up in our cells, that they left us unsupervised.

Ten days before Christmas, and after eighteen days in JDC, the judge placed me back in the custody of Mom. Getting out of JDC was like a honeymoon that consisted of eating a lot of KFC. I feel a lot of sweetness toward Mom thinking about my first week out of JDC because she went to the Dollar Tree in the mall and bought and wrapped so many presents the tree was full underneath, all around. Mom was never too good at wrapping presents or keeping traditions, but this Christmas she tried to make it especially memorable.

Two days before Christmas, we appeared in court to determine how I'd be charged for hitting Mom. While waiting to be called into the courtroom, a woman approached me and introduced herself as my *guardian ad litem*—something those in the foster system call a "GAL, or in some states CASA, a *court appointed special advocate*." I followed her as she directed me toward a room where we could talk alone. Before she asked me the first question, a loud banging erupted through the door. We looked at each other afraid, unsure why someone would knock so aggressively.

She carefully and slowly opened the door to see my mom on the other side fuming. "You cannot speak to my daughter. You cannot take her by herself. She is a minor and I am her mother, and I demand that you not speak to her alone!"

The suited woman swung the door open, looked at Mom and said, "No ma'am. This is her right. Now excuse me." My GAL directed me to follow her to the next room as she marched right past Mom, but Mom continued following us around while demanding that I not be spoken to alone and that I be charged for beating a disabled person, referring to herself. After many attempts to hide ourselves in various corners of the courthouse, my GAL and I found ourselves in a closet, standing toe to toe, surrounded by boxes and cabinets of orange filing folders, a scene I'd soon become familiar with. Once the outside of the room remained quiet for some time, my GAL promised me I could tell her the truth with no consequences.

I wanted to tell her the truth because I didn't want to live with Mom, but I was scared that if I did tell her the truth and Mom found out and I was placed back with Mom, the abuse, outbursts, and fights would become worse than ever before. I took the chance and sobbed as I told my GAL about the abuse, the drugs, the times I helped Mom check into the coping center after a manic episode and sobbed harder when I told her about the words Mom spoke over me.

She quickly wrote on a yellow notepad and thanked me for being brave. When my GAL shut her binder, I believed I'd be shutting the chapter of living with Mom. She opened the door, and I believed stepping out of the door meant stepping out of abuse. Leaving the filing closet meant leaving Mom's house. My sister and I could live with Tonya. My sister would have another sister her age. We'd have a hot tub and a Mom who spoke kindly to us.

But reassurance left me when I saw Mom sitting on a chair just to the right of the door. Fear and anxiety came back to take its place and shot through my entire body. I remembered Mom's threats about taking me out of this world as fast as she brought me into it. I was sure if I went home that might be the case. She shot up and her nose nearly touched my GAL's. She swore I was a boy crazy liar who only wanted to leave her house because I didn't want to follow her rules. If my GAL believed her and I had to go back with Mom, my life would be worse. I replayed Mom's threats in my head over and over again, "You think things are bad now. They will only get worse if you tell."

The GAL chucked her folder and notes at the ground and started screaming back. She called Mom crazy, said my case was too crazy for anyone to take, and then abruptly left the courthouse.

A caseworker who must have heard the scene quickly grabbed me and directed me away from Mom. I was to wait in the courtroom. By myself. Alone, I sat in anticipation of any answer to ease the crushing weight. Still today, I hate when a group of people are together without me, making plans. I despise when people whisper in the same room as me. It almost never fails to remind me of the countless times I sat outside of offices and courtrooms while people who rarely asked my opinion made plans about my life.

In foster care, foster youth rarely have any control over their cases. Foster youth are often viewed as incompetent and troubled. It is believed by caseworkers, county workers, judges, and others that they can't make decisions for themselves so they are never given the opportunity, which results in kids becoming adults and being unable to make decisions for themselves.

One of the most powerful ways we can serve foster youth is giving them a say. Hearing them. And letting them hear what is said in the meetings, because when we don't know what's said, we often imagine, and our trauma tends to make what we imagine worse than reality.

There were so many voices determining what was next in my life, yet I had no voice in the matter. I sat in the courtroom, tracing the mural on the wall with my fingers, and the waiting felt like it went on forever.

A social worker eventually entered the room and told me the judge decided Mom was mentally unstable and it was evident that she had something to hide. I was relieved to hear that they determined that the next best thing for me was to enter the foster care system.

I suggested I live with Tonya, but the caseworker said Tonya wasn't an option. Though this was the case, I was still excited and hopeful that my sister and I would end up in a family that loved us and would take good care of us.

For holiday's sake, caseworkers held off placing me in a foster home and allowed me and my sister to spend Christmas with Tonya and her family. Somehow Tonya gathered presents for my sister and me to open alongside her two children. We were actually given more presents between the two of us than the four members of Tonya's family had all together.

This is a foster-care phenomenon—where youth in foster care receive more presents than biological children because people so generously want to donate to the foster children. Though I trust people have good intentions when it comes to giving to foster youth, I think our society has viewed foster children as charity cases for far too long.

Foster youth and former foster youth need more help than other youth because of their lack of family. To former foster youth, community is like family, and my communities have helped me immensely to be where I am today. However, I do feel if we are going to pay for an entire medical procedure, we must teach the foster youth how to apply for and maintain the best medical insurance. If we are going to furnish an entire apartment, we must teach young men and women how to apply for jobs, offer them the skills it takes to keep jobs, and maybe even teach them how to build their own furniture and be wise with their finances. Too many people throw money and goods at vulnerable youth when they need time, basic skills, and long-term relationships.

I didn't want to be treated like a charity. I wanted to be invested in. If we want to see our foster youth empowered, we must grant them responsibility. I want vulnerable youth to have what they need for today, but more than that, I want vulnerable youth to obtain the skills they need for their families tomorrow.

~ * * ~

Picking through all of my Christmas presents, I asked Tonya if we could return the gifts for different colors and exchange what was unwanted for things bigger and better. I was looking forward to moving into a new room and wanted a cute bedspread and decorations. So with a cartful of gifts, Tonya patiently waited in the long line at Walmart returns the day after Christmas.

As an adult, I realized how ungrateful I must have appeared, and I asked Tonya why she let me return the gifts, instead of using the situation as an opportunity to teach me a lesson on gratefulness. She said simply, "I knew that's not what you needed. That wouldn't have communicated love to you in that moment." Tonya always took chances to imbue love, knowing lessons sink deep when shown instead of spoken.

I didn't want to leave. But when it was time to take the lights down and throw the Christmas tree out, it was time for us to leave Tonya's. My sister and I moved a few counties away to live with Donna, a foster mom of decades who displayed a picture of every child she had ever fostered on the wall in her hallway.

Twelve people lived in the home, including her biological children, adopted children, emancipated adults, grandchildren, and foster children. The room my sister and I slept in looked like the orphanage in the movie *Annie*. Each bed lined up after the other, with a total of ten beds in one room. The mattresses were thin and the bed frames were metal. I could hear the walls scream, "In it for the money!" Though this was the case, I actually don't think most foster families are in it for the stipend, but I think it can easily become a motivation. For some time, I started to believe that foster parents weren't paid enough because that's what I always heard. But when I eventually became a foster parent myself, I thought the stipend was more than enough.

I've served in child welfare for nearly ten years, and I think what I witnessed we have to guard against the most in this field is letting apathy take over. It's difficult because we have to remain levelheaded and stable in this midst of instability for the children and families we serve. But I think the calm demeanor we feel we have to maintain easily gets entangled with not thinking how a room like the one my sister and I were in might make a child feel. I think, over time, Donna grew apathetic.

Donna smoked in the kitchen while the older girls taught me how to huff hair spray. I was glad not to pay as much attention to my sister and hang out with girls my age, but whenever I was with my sister in front of Donna, Donna demanded me to stop "playing the parent." I wasn't trying to play parent; I just didn't think she needed to eat when she wasn't hungry.

Mom never forced us to eat all of our food off of our plates. She said when we were full we could be done eating, and if we didn't like something after we tried it, we could choose a healthy substitute or go without it. Donna wanted us to eat everything off of our plate, all of the time, and we didn't choose our own servings. To save my sister, I'd usually eat her food when Donna wasn't looking and then reassure her that it was okay that she wasn't hungry. Donna argued I was acting like a mom.

~ * * * ~

During my next court date, I was assigned a new GAL. She was a soft-spoken woman named Tammy. It turned out her oldest son was in my class, and her husband was one of my teachers. Though she was gentle, she aimed to be serious when she spoke to me.

"I know what your last GAL said. That wasn't right. I am here for you. I am for you. And I will not leave you until this case is over. I am here to stay." I didn't really know what the implications of her saying that were then, but I do now.

Everyone in my caseload came and went at one point or another. Except Tammy. She stayed. She was the only person in my caseload who didn't leave throughout my 1,544 days in foster care.

Tammy's job description was "to advocate for what was in the best interest of the child." That was the first time I'd ever heard the word "advocate." And I knew I wanted to follow in her footsteps. I thought I'd go to college for law, and I'd be just like her. An advocate who stayed.

Chapter 9

LABELED

picked out an outfit for my sissy, laid it on the empty bed next to hers, and hugged her every night before bed. Her big light blue eyes and soft cheekbones were enough to make me smile after days that felt empty.

But my heart sank when she told me Kevin, the biological son of Donna, abused her.

Almost immediately, I said, "We have to tell somebody," mistakenly, repeating the same words Mom told me after I was abused, and I knew I scared my sister. I tried to change my approach, "We don't *have* to tell anybody." I said in a panic. Then I quickly asked, "What do *you* want to do about it?"

"I don't want to," she replied.

~ * * * ~

The next morning at school, I stole a classmate's phone out of her locker to call Tonya. I felt so desolate in the large bathroom stall, but I wanted to be alone, and made sure no one else was in the restroom when I called. I started to cry as I left the voicemail. "She says she doesn't want to tell anybody. I don't know what to do. Maybe you can help me figure out what to do. I'll try calling you back later. I love you. Bye."

Just a couple hours later I was called into the principal's office where two caseworkers sat. The caseworkers started their investigation with asking me questions, but they appeared fed up with my answers before I even started answering them. "So, what did your sister tell you?"

I didn't want to repeat the words Allison told me. Just thinking about them made me feel nasty. So I came up with different words and watered-down phrases that I felt communicated what my sister told me. They continued to ask me questions, and I answered as I felt able, until the case worker slammed her binder.

"We're done here. Your story just keeps changing."

I shook my head from side to side and shot up. "No. I just didn't want to say the words." Flustered and overwhelmed, I cried, "I don't know. I don't know how to say it."

They got up and left, and I was directed back to class. It was over.

So instead of focusing on school, I focused on making a plan. It was my responsibility to keep me and my sister safe and surviving.

I'd go back to Donna's and keep a better eye on my sister and Kevin from here on out. Playing mom was necessary at this point, and I needed to be better if I wanted Allison to be safe.

When I arrived back at Donna's that evening, my caseworkers and sister sat at the high-top counter between the kitchen and living room. My caseworker held a garbage bag in her right hand.

"What's going on?" I asked

"You can't stay here, Tori."

Noticing my confusion, she elaborated.

"You can't just lie about something like this and expect families to keep you."

"I didn't lie! Allison tell them!" I said aggressively.

My sister sat silently. Tears streamed down my face. My sister didn't look at me. I tried to speak calmer. "Sissy, tell them. You can tell them."

I repeated exactly what I remembered her telling me.

My caseworker exclaimed, "See! Your story changed again!"

I tried to argue my case that I didn't want to say the words, but I'd say them to keep my sister safe. Ignoring my pleas, my caseworker grabbed the garbage bag and walked toward the door. "At this point, you're not placeable. There's no family that will take you with these kinds of behaviors, Tori."

I didn't have the "behaviors" other foster youth I met did. I didn't sneak out, blow up, or self-harm. I was never diagnosed with a mental illness, nor was I ever violent, but I realized I wasn't going to change anything.

"I need to pack our things," I said with my head down.

"I have your things right here," my caseworker gestured toward the garbage bag.

I wiped my tears, picked my sister up, and walked toward the door. "I can carry the bag."

I remember the scene precisely. It felt like the house came crumbling on top of me, like no matter how many times I tried to close my eyes and open them up again, I had to accept this was not just another night terror. This bull called life that completely crushed my ribs and trampled on top of me would last for years, but it started when my caseworker said, "Allison is staying here."

Appearing strong was the only option I had. I might have had no control over my circumstances, but I could control my strength and emotions, even though the grief felt immovable, like the horns of a bull had pinned me to the side of an arena.

~ * * * ~

The strangers who puppeted my life heard more clearly the crinkles of the trash bag holding my belongings than they did my cries. I couldn't have cared less about carrying around a garbage bag. What I wanted was to be heard.

The first duffle bag I received was purple, which was my least favorite color because it reminded me of Barney, which made the color feel immature. The stuffed dog was a better fit for a five-year-old than a fifteen-year-old. Suave shampoo and conditioner that had a yellow, $1, Dollar General sticker on the front of the bottle was bundled in the bag, as if any black or mixed kid could use it without hair breakage.

Valuable resources were wasted time and time again on bags full of things I could not use because they were not what I needed. And it is baffling how easily people are persuaded to throw money at causes and organizations making money off of foster youth vulnerabilities. The program that supplied this bag is a seven-million-dollar nonprofit that is not even considering the ethnic differences of youth's hair, giving foster youth stuff they can't even use. Seven million dollars.

And the saddest part is those same organizations convince youth that they need a good suitcase more than they need to be heard. The people claiming to be the heroes in foster care are the same people, unknowingly and sometimes even knowingly, keeping the cycle of foster care fueled. Helping foster youth has become more about nonprofit logos, branding, titles; and we all know, for many, it's "about the money." I say this not out of anger but out of love for my brothers and sisters in the foster care system. I want them to be seen for the purpose-driven and empathetic people God has made them to be, rather than a charity case.

Listening to foster youth is scary because it means we might actually have to change something about ourselves. It's easier to buy something for the poor orphan, to make ourselves feel better, than it is to give our time to vulnerable populations and *actually* figure out what they need. It's easier to throw suitcases and pay for Disneyland trips because when the community service and the vacation are over, you can go back to acting like the corrupt system and all the lonely children in it don't exist.

I want you to hear me. A company doesn't have to give me a suitcase for me to know I am worth more than a garbage bag. I'm not saying that providing for needs is bad. I'm saying some of the corrupt companies out there need to stop exploiting people like me to earn a million dollar "nonprofit" income and take the time to find out what the actual needs are. I'm saying some companies are too scared to help in a way that is effective because they don't want to work themselves out of a cushy career.

~ * * * ~

The investigation of my sister's abuse was brushed under the rug, and my sister remained in the home for a bit longer. Not wanting to worry or retraumatize Mom, caseworkers had to come up with a believable reason for this new development, and so they told her they had to separate me and Allison because *I* hurt her. Files and papers deemed me manipulative and a liar.

I will never forget what I heard in the car from the caseworkers. I still wonder if they said it to upset me or if they were having a conversation they believed I couldn't hear.

"Donna is so awesome. I love her," one of them said casually in conversation.

I still wonder, Did they love her? Or did they love that she could house twelve plus kids? Did they love her, or did they love the fact that Donna's yes sent them home from work earlier? Did they love her, or did they love her willingness to turn a blind eye?

Vexation shook me to the core. I was not a liar nor a manipulator, and I wouldn't understand for years why I was deemed one.

I didn't see it then, but I see now how difficult being a caseworker is. When twelve people are living under one roof with proven abuse, every child in danger needs a new home. How does a caseworker find homes in a small rural county for so many children? They can't. There aren't enough homes and families, so they turn a blind eye to abuse disclosures and continue "loving" the foster parents who will house children.

How do you terminate abusive homes when you don't want children to be homeless? How do you take away a foster parent's license when your annual quota requires you to maintain and gain a certain amount of licensed foster parents? How do you advocate for what is in the best interest of the child when you are advocating for the government? You can't, which leaves some of the most struggling kids in America suffering at the hands of the government.

This is how the cycle of abuse and neglect continues. Children are put into homes that are meant to keep them safe. Instead they are sometimes, yet again, abused. These children can't form relationships or bonds with others. Their trauma overtakes them. They birth their own children and can't form bonds with them. They've never been taught how to, and every time they open their eyes, they see the residue of their trauma. They abuse their own children because it's their only version of normal, and so on. If we want to break the cycle of abuse and neglect, investigations must be conducted thoroughly.

Another one of our problems is that we execute short-term solutions. A common short-term solution in the foster care system is to place children in safer homes, even if those homes are overpopulated and not necessarily safe.

In many counties across the nation, each foster family has a limit of children they can house; however, that limit is based on how many beds the parents have in the home. Some counties do a parent-to-child ratio and stick to the rules, but many times caseworkers make exceptions to that rule, and families are allowed to have more children in the home, again, simply based on the number of beds in the house.

This way of placing children is efficient for caseworkers; however, in the long run, this form of placement is ineffective because foster parents are housing more children than they can take care of or supervise. This is especially dangerous when dealing with children who need more time and attention because of the trauma and neglect they've experienced. When we place children to fill beds, we are creating a system of temporary housing rather than a long-term solution of finding children their forever, safe, and loving families.

It is crucial that each foster child receives the attention, services, and care they need to heal from their abuse, neglect, and trauma. One stay-at-home mom cannot drive children to counseling, carefully handle sensory issues, help children who are behind in school with their homework, be patiently understanding during a meltdown, and assure there is not abuse occurring behind closed doors with twelve children in her home. And no foster mom or dad should be expected to do so. While there is a technical limit of how many children each foster family can have placed in their home, that limit needs to be enforced instead of ignored for convenience sake.

In my opinion, the limits that currently exist, even on a technical level, should change. I think the limit should not be based on beds or even a parent-to-child ratio, but on an Adverse Childhood Experiences (ACEs), trauma, and behavior scale. For example, when I went into the foster care system, I generally did well in school, but I never attended counseling, and anyone who knew anything about psychology would say it was pretty evident I had some kind of anxiety disorder and should have attended therapy. I could have still been placed with a couple of children who tested higher on the scale and receive the care I needed.

Later in foster care, I was housed with young women who needed extra care and attention but were housed with nine other young women and were never able to receive the attention they truly needed to move forward healing.

Imagine this perceived scale ranging from zero to five hundred, with several different factors about where a child is in education, how the child has been traumatized, experience in counseling, and so on adding to a child's number; and when a single household hits the five hundred mark, whether they have only one child or six, they cannot house any more children until a child they are housing moves down the scale (experiences a great deal of healing). And children should be able to move down the scale. The foster care system should not solely be used to house children but should be used to help them heal.

In my mind's eye, I see a family that could have been licensed for four kids. But given the specific situation, let's say they hit the five hundred mark with one youth in foster care or two. In my view, the door should close, simply because their capacity to genuinely care for the children in their home has hit its ceiling. This sort of scaling system would allow for a lot more healing for the kids in the homes and a lot less burnout for the foster parents. And, over time, a lot more successful reports for the caseworker, too. Imagine that. Healing.

Chapter 10

SOFTENED

The tall brick buildings looked eerie in the dark after the hour drive from Donna's. You may have heard that orphanages do not exist in America. But they do. We've just changed the name to save face and to maintain the narrative that we do everything better. Modern-day American orphanages are called "group homes," "residential facilities," or "filling homes." One in seven foster children live in an institutional setting such as these, and 40 percent of foster teens in group homes have no clinical reason (such as a behavioral issue or diagnosed mental disorder) to be placed in these institutions, other than that they cannot live with their biological family.[1]

Much research has been done about the failings of institutions. It is absolutely crucial for the development of children that they are living in families rather than facilities. While I wouldn't abolish group homes, I wouldn't advocate for too many. Group homes are for children with acute clinical needs that need rehabilitated to prepare for adoption and permanency. A residential home I've experienced doing godly healing work is Big Oak Ranch in Springville, Alabama. It was founded by John Croyle. And another is House of Providence, founded by Maggie and Jay Dunn. I believe the success is rooted in the heart of these founders seeking the kingdom of heaven above all else, but founders and facilities like these are few and far between.

At the campus we drove onto, there were three group homes. One for young men who had behavioral and mental issues, another for young men who had been sex offenders, and the third was a home for young women with behavioral and mental issues.

My caseworkers met with group home staff behind a closed door. Anxiety rushed through my veins as if it replaced my blood. At some point, anxiety became my first emotional reaction. I wondered what they would say about me and what consequences might ensue. People who had a lot of control over my life would be talking about me . . . without me . . . again.

Staff treated me like an object to be itemized rather than a human to be nurtured. My garbage bag was emptied onto the ground so my property could be "inventoried." It makes sense, because many group homes are like businesses, and children are their products. Any successful business must take inventory. So we counted and recorded every item onto a sheet of paper that was filed away. Before sending me to bed, I was given a clipboard with a point sheet on it where I would write and track my behaviors. The staff awarded me my first positive points because I was compliant to head to bed, which had never been an issue in the first place.

****

The following morning, when I saw the other girls, I was taken back. They formed a line as the staff prepared to hand out their medications. They appeared zombified. I assume because most of them were over medicated. To my surprise, cameras were hooked up in nearly every corner.

The first night I did not think I qualified to be in the group home, but after seeing all that, I knew I didn't. I'd never been on psychiatric medication before, despite having a mandatory psychological evaluation when I entered foster care. My general behaviors were not ones that needed to be highly monitored. And I had been in only one foster home during this time in foster care. The reality is my caseworker did not want to do the hard work of finding me a family home that night.

The behavioral school on campus made academics uninspiring. I had a 4.0 the previous semester of my eighth-grade year, and suddenly I was being given math problems and reading assignments I could have completed in the fifth grade. When lessons and assignments were more challenging, they were difficult to comprehend and complete in the classroom because it was not uncommon for my peers to chuck desks across the room or burst out screaming.

I find it interesting that we expect and hope for underserved populations to thrive this way. We often place them in environments where they aren't being challenged and where they can continue to live in victimhood instead of placing them in areas where they can grow by seeing their peers thriving and being pushed in their abilities. Their talents are never able to grow because they aren't in environments where that's possible.

Thankfully, I didn't remain here. After some time I got a new caseworker who saw that I attended public school because of my excelling grades, behaviors, and probably because of my nagging, daily phone calls, and begging to go to school off campus. I was the first girl in the group home in nearly ten years who was allowed to attend public school.

While most girls in the home received multiple higher level "point losses" in a single day, it was surprising if I even received one low level "point loss." If I did receive a negative point, I replayed in my head what I did wrong and how I could do better next time. While other girls tended to blow up and get violent when they received point losses, I secluded myself, cried, and beat myself up with the same demeaning words my mom used toward me. I'd replay the scenario in my head and even journal how I could do better next time.

On most days, at the end of the day, the staff would realize they hadn't "taught" me anything or "given" me any points for an entire day because they were so consumed with actually monitoring behaviors with other girls. So after the girls went to bed, they'd make up points and fill out my point sheet.

~ * * * ~

Going to church was another activity that allowed me to be out of the house. It was a great encouragement and inspiration to me. Hearing that there was a plan and purpose for my life kept me going. Hearing stories of inspirational Christians and disciples made me want to be kinder to the girls who lived in my house. I even considered forgiving

Mom. Somewhere along the way I started asking myself how my life might have been a blessing rather than a curse.

~ * * * ~

I've recently changed my mind about mental illness. I prefer to call it a mental weakness and rejoice over the fact that God's strength is made perfect in my weakness. I also feel that what the world sees as a flaw, God sees as beautiful. And what the world says we should shut up behind closed doors, or even overmedicate, God wants to bring out into the light and use for His glory. I am more artistic and creative because of my mind. I am more thoughtful and aware because of my mind. I am more observant, risky, and yet safe because of my mind. It's a beautiful contradiction, and it is the way God has fearfully and wonderfully made me. Now trauma is one of the reasons my brain works the way it does, and hear me say I'd never wish trauma on a person just so their brain could operate in some unique way. My point is that God has the ability to turn something evil into something good, and my mind is evidence of that.

As an adult, seeking whole healing, I have learned about this cool thing called synaptic pruning, which occurs in the brain between early childhood and adulthood. During synaptic pruning, the brain eliminates extra synapses. So in this process, the brain removes connections that are no longer needed. I feel that this time in my life—when I started to be more attentive at church and when I was put in leadership roles at the group home and at school—was God's way of telling me that I am fearfully and wonderfully made, even my mind, which the world would call ill.

It is a mystery to me when I started to realize I was a leader and a role model, but I do think it started while living in the group home. Following the services at church, a single mom regularly came up to me with her daughter. Her daughter was mixed and—though I didn't realize it then, still having some confusion about my racial identity—the little girl looked a lot like me. We could have easily passed as sisters.

That little girl made me feel special when she walked over to me just to sit with me through the church service or when she ran up to me to give me a hug before I left the church. During special church events we'd play together all evening. Her mom continued to affirm in me that I was her greatest role model, and when they went home, her little girl asked about when she would see me next.

Then in the spring I was allowed to run track, which made it so that I was out of the house for most of the day. I felt like the nine other girls I lived with were jealous of me, and rightfully so. Though we used to open our windows that were right next to each other, and talk until late into the night, while we were supposed to be in bed, we stopped doing that because I wanted to sleep well to run well and have energy for school. Naturally, since I wasn't there often, my relationships with the girls faded. On most days, I played my part in the group home. I attended counseling, said okay even when I disagreed—just like the staff taught me, earned my points, and acted friendly. But I did so only so I could complete the program and leave.

Once school was over, I was required to start attending "group" counseling. A young girl named Jenni, who smashed the frame that held a picture of my sister and me and wiped her poop on walls when she was angry, shared her story as the group listened intently.

After living in several foster homes, she was adopted, until the adoption was terminated because the alcoholic father was caught brutally abusing her. My heart broke because I didn't even know adoptions could be broken, but my heart soared when she started speaking about her restored hope after she was adopted again. Then she proceeded to talk about how her second set of adopted parents sex trafficked her so they would receive two means of income: financial assistance from the government for fostering and adopting her and the second from her exploitation. I felt angry at her parents. Angry at the home we lived in because it wasn't what she needed. She needed a family to love her. And I was angry at myself for judging her instead of seeking to understand her.

Jenni's story stirred something in my spirit. Jenni's story combined with what I'd heard from church started a building of understanding. We have empathy when we understand that hurt people hurt people.

And we help ourselves and others when we understand that healed people heal people.

Oftentimes, the worse the youth's story was—the more sexual trauma they'd experienced, the more severe the torture and abuse were—the worse their behaviors were. And their behaviors were bad because their behaviors stemmed from their psychological and biological reactions to trauma.

I was so focused on myself, not even caring to listen to the stories of the people I slept in the same house with, I had missed out on how these girls could help heal me with their own stories. The girls weren't the problem. They were the solution. Talking to them late into the night wasn't going to be the reason I was locked away in a group home forever. Listening to them and loving them was my way to freedom.

During the first week after I arrived at the group home, I attended a counseling session for the first time in my life. My counselor was a petite woman who spoke seriously. "You're quiet. You're a good girl. Your record isn't bad, huh? So, why are you here?" I shrugged my shoulders because I didn't know. And I know now, that's exactly why I was there. Because I didn't know what I didn't know. The counseling, the stable adults, and the young women I lived with would make me more aware.

Jenni's story and Jesus's story inspired me. As I stepped into the genesis of my healing journey, I wanted to do whatever work in myself necessary to contribute to healing, not hurting. So when I was supposed to have my lights off and be in bed, I knocked on one of the girl's walls and talked to her through the vent. Though notes were prohibited, because they could easily be unsupervised, I wrote Bible verses in notes and traded them with girls until we were caught and disciplined. Instead of staying longer than I needed at track practice, I'd come home to play Rock Band with my housemates. Just a few weeks ago, I received a message from one of the girls that said she still had the Bible I gave her with the note I wrote to her in it, which I don't even remember. Things like this make me know that God was with me and the Holy Spirit was working throughout my entire life.

He changed the perspective of my heart to be more like His. In each of the young women, I saw Mom as a young girl being trafficked and abused, which helped me forgive Mom and understand that her unhealed trauma was the cause for much of mine. And while I didn't have to take responsibility for the trauma caused to me, I did need to take responsibility for my own healing and deciding what I would do about it. This is what caused me to embrace counseling and the process of the group home even though I still do not completely agree with their methods.

Throughout this process, my empathy grew, and I understood people and myself more than I had before. When I spoke, people told me I had wisdom beyond my years. Still, people tell me this. And while I don't know if I'd agree about the wisdom part, I believe meeting and listening to so many people from so many different walks of life at such a young age has given me empathy beyond my years.

The chains I was easily entangled in when Mom's verbal abuses repeated themselves in my head were broken quicker when I thought, *She didn't mean that. And not even she knows it.* Forgiveness took the key out of my transgressor's hands and placed it in my own. I was the prisoner and the guard. Finally, I had the power to set myself free, and that freedom made me softer.

Soon enough, most of the girls stopped envying me and started looking up to me. A staff member said, "I've never seen a group of girls this well behaved." Another staff member looked at me and said, "I've never seen a group of girls so well led." May we not underestimate one person's story and one person's behaviors. They have the power to change an entire culture.

Chapter 11

DAMAGED

Nearly a year had gone by at the group home, and I'd completed the program, but no one told me where I would go next. Since I once sneaked a peak at my file and read in large, bold and red letters, "NO CONTACT: TONYA BRISENO," I sadly accepted that living with Tonya would not be an option. Though caseworkers knew I wouldn't ever live with Mom again, Mom never lost her parental rights, which put me in a unique situation that is referred to as a Permanent Placement Living Arrangement or PPLA in Ohio. But since Mom kept her parental rights, she demanded out of jealousy that the one place I could never live was Tonya's.

Every day felt like a waiting game.

~ * * ~

Denzel was an athletic, handsome black man married to Sarah, who was a soft-spoken, beautiful white woman. Denzel was a psychiatrist and Sarah was a math teacher. Together, they coached eighth-grade track. And though I did not resemble their son, Jude, or daughter, Callie, as a mixed girl, I did resemble Denzel and Sarah in some ways. When I started hanging out with their family, everyone assumed I was their daughter, and I wished I were.

Sarah and Denzel felt like the perfect people to be my parents. But they weren't certified foster parents, and my caseworkers said I needed to come back to the county to be close to Mom, though we knew reunification was no longer an option. Mom was too unstable, and though foster care wasn't a walk in the park, I couldn't fathom the idea of living with Mom again.

After months of waiting for answers, I sat in the happiest meeting I'd ever been a part of. My caseworkers and GAL informed me that Denzel and Sarah were in the process of becoming certified foster parents just for me. There was no dream I wanted to come true more than this one.

The licensing process felt like it took a century, but as soon as they were licensed, I moved in with them. They let me paint my room whatever colors I wanted—a gaudy hot pink and spray-painted silver, if you're dying to know. They also let me be in their family pictures and Christmas cards, which proved to me they believed I was there to stay. Everyone believed undoubtedly this is where I would grow up and come home to for the rest of my life.

Out of all of the foster families I lived with before and after, this family was the only one I loved this intensely. And I wouldn't have questioned that they loved me more than I did them.

We had plenty of conflict. I was a faster runner than Callie, replacing her on a relay team, which caused a lot of tension in the home. With so much grace, Sarah and Denzel explained to me that they were equally proud of us and loved us for who we were and not for what we did or did not do. Denzel had tattooed Callie and Jude's names on his arm but not mine, and I didn't understand why he wouldn't just add my name once I moved in. Sarah explained to me that tattoos were permanent and though they wanted me to be permanent there were outside factors like my mom and the caseworkers who had more control over permanency, so for now, a tattoo was not an option. It was difficult to understand in the moment, and it did hurt, but I look back now and understand why they did what they did.

I'm sure there were even more conflicts from their perspective, but their continual reassurance about their love for me and their transparency about the dynamics of our family made it the only foster home where I felt like I belonged wholeheartedly.

~ * * * ~

I was fourteen, but when I grabbed Denzel's hand to hold it, it was innocent. I felt like a little girl holding her daddy's hand, which I hadn't had the chance to do since Issac and Mom married, and Issac wasn't really one for hand-holding anyway. But Denzel proudly held my hand whenever I grabbed it. He knew I was making up for a fatherly love that was lost before I was even born. But the foster care agency told Sarah that holding Denzel's hand was inappropriate and it had to stop immediately.

When I think of this time, I think of that famous "Pieces" song, which speaks of a pure, fatherly love that isn't ashamed—a love that is proud to be seen with the likes of me.

That's what Denzel's love was like. He didn't care what others thought about how my trauma manifested. His intent was to be a part of the healing of it. To hold my hand until I stopped holding his, naturally, like little girls do. Sarah and Denzel handled the situation the best way they could have. They were honest.

"The agency says you and Denzel have to stop holding hands. It isn't because we think it's bad. They just don't want anyone, you or Denzel, to be perceived wrong or get into trouble. We know it is innocent, and we wish we could just let it stop naturally, as I am sure it would, but we have to abide by their rules, or else they could take our foster care license away."

These rules are the petty rules county agencies enforce in foster homes they visit once a month. Though foster parents are in a better place to know what is best for their foster children, the caseworkers' voices, rules, and regulations win nearly every time.

Though Sarah couldn't have worded it better than she did, I was embarrassed. I realized I was too old to hold Denzel's hand. And more so, I was embarrassed that people were sexualizing something I did. I felt nasty and wanted to hide my face. It made me feel like once again, people were sexualizing me. It felt like no matter what I did, even when out of Mom's care, I was destined for sexual promiscuity. And at that point I viewed my body and reputation as damaged goods. I felt like there was no point of abstaining from sex when the whole world already viewed me as sexual.

~ * * * ~

At the group home we weren't taught about character or integrity when no one was looking, nor were we given opportunities to be unsupervised. There was not a chance to make a mistake without being docked points. Fearing the criticism, I avoided any points of conflict, which made it difficult to learn. If I learned anything, it was only how not to get in trouble, and I did so by watching the other girls, not by learning my own innate faults and tendencies. The program did not teach me how to ask questions about life or how to speak up for myself. Instead it taught me how to respond by saying, "Okay," even if there was a reasonable disagreement to be had. Because if I didn't, I'd receive "negative points."

By the time I left the group home, it had been over a year since I had been out of intense oversight by an adult. I anxiously anticipated being securely locked up with cameras watching my every move, which played a large role in my rebellion. Each chance to be unsupervised made me a glutton for fun.

Drugs and alcohol never enticed me because I'd seen the damage it did to families, but I didn't know the damage that could be done by continuing not to ask questions and say "okay." I was staying out late, making out with boys, and skinny-dipping at the local campsite. Word started to come back to Denzel and Sarah that I was being rowdy, and as sweetly as they could they handled each situation. Giving me discipline, overcommunicating their love for me, and granting me the same freedom they granted their children after consequences, I believe, because they wanted to be fair. They didn't want to make me feel like the "foster daughter." They wanted to make me feel like their "daughter."

And though I felt like their daughter, I rarely felt like a sister. Being brother and sister through foster care rarely makes anyone feel like a biological brother and sister, especially if ages are close. Jude and I wanted to love each other like we were siblings because we knew it was our family that was at stake. We were keenly aware of our boundaries, until one night we weren't.

Feeling loved was my motivation, and I had a thought that if I could get Jude to love me, and maybe even want to marry me someday just by doing what he asked, then I would be able to be a part of the family forever. But I knew what we did together was wrong.

Shame compelled me to write the details in my journal, which Sarah read when I wasn't home. I was told I would temporarily relocate to a respite home as decisions were being made. Before the temporary removal, Denzel came into my room. I was looking down at the turtle they bought me, to be fair, after they got Callie her dog.

Denzel squeezed me tight. "Don't worry. You'll always be our girl. We'll figure this out." His words comforted me, and I carried them to the closed-door meeting the following week.

~ * * * ~

I'd had a few foster sisters who had to take the morning-after pill. What I understood about it at the time was that it would prevent pregnancy, not terminate a life. The caseworkers suggested I take it and convinced me that if I did, I would be more likely to remain a part of Sarah and Denzel's family. I stayed quiet and took long, hot showers to comfort myself and ease the pain when the bleeding and cramps persisted.

What was even more painful was days later, when my caseworker finally walked out of the hour-long, closed-door meeting, and told me I couldn't go back. "This wasn't Denzel and Sarah's decision. This is county policy." The words were a surprise to me. I'd waited a long time in the transition home for an answer. If it was county policy, why wouldn't they have told me sooner? The entire time I believed I was headed back to my family. I'd taken the pill, and we'd taken time away from each other. Denzel promised we would figure it all out, but instead we were experiencing a fallout.

I ran downstairs, unable to catch my breath as each sob caught in my chest. I said sorry so many times, like maybe an apology would turn back time. There was nothing I wanted more than to be with this family. My counselor picked me up off of the floor to hold me until I had no other choice than to let the emotions cease.

For months after, I prayed the county would make an exception if they saw me doing well. Like I'd earned most things, I'd earn my way back home.

During an annual court hearing, the prosecutor said I'd "forced" my twelve-year-old foster brother to have sex with me. As usual, I wasn't permitted to speak in court. My caseworkers and lawyers were supposed to speak on my behalf. I wanted to say that he was *not* forced, *nor was he twelve*. He was just months younger than me. But the conversation in court went on for much too long until my GAL was finally given the opportunity to tell the truth of the story.

The truth was known by some, but for the most part, myself and Denzel and Sarah's family didn't talk about it, which caused people to imagine what happened, and rumors spread, which made me readily defend Jude.

Thankfully, when I finally emancipated out of the foster care system years later, I became close to Sarah again. She'd take me out for ice cream and dinner, buy me Christmas presents each year, and talk with me for hours. Both she and Denzel even attended my college graduation and sat at the front of my wedding. In an earthly sense, I feel they are the epitome of God's forgiveness. Though the mistake we made cost us a family made whole, their love for me was unreserved. Even when rumors spread about their family and son, they were proud to be seen with me. Even when it pained Sarah to see me and leave me each time we visited, expressing every time that she wished I could have been theirs, their love remained wild for me.

Chapter 12

FAVORITED

In foster care, I rarely knew why my caseworkers made the decisions they did. I moved back to the county where Mom lived, and sadly, my caseworker changed again. Supervision at my new foster home, Pauline's, was intense. When she went to work in the morning, my foster sister, Emile, and I had to hang out at the neighbors two hours before the bus arrived. We weren't allowed to have social media or any technology, though Emile had an iPod only to be used for music. I think because Pauline was so tired when she returned from her factory job, she spent a majority of her time on her own computer scrolling through Facebook.

Emile was smart—one of the smartest girls I'd ever lived with, and she would somehow sneak to find the WiFi password at anyone's house and hook it up to her iPod. We wouldn't text or call anyone while at Pauline's to prevent her from finding out, but we did when we were at the neighbor's in the morning.

Eventually the neighbor's son found out, and while I was at the table doing my homework, he said he'd tell his mom and Pauline that we were using the WiFi if I didn't "do stuff with him." So I did, for months. And if I'm completely honest, I thought I was receiving attention; I felt wanted for the first time in a long time. I thought maybe if I was good enough at the acts, we could secretly date, and we'd be secretly in love. Looking back, I realize the young girl I was, lacking any sort of spiritual shepherding around what sexuality even is and how God factors into what we do with our bodies—the wonderful good we can do with them and the not so good, depending on the context. And I also roll my eyes that we went to the neighbor's every morning to be supervised, when we probably would have been better off at home. The parents of the house slept all morning, and their son was the same age as us—which we knew from my last placement—I didn't do so well with.

Eventually, Pauline caught on that Emile was using the iPod with WiFi on it, and we got it taken away. We had no idea what to do with ourselves as teenage girls who couldn't go anywhere or have social media, so once I started running track again. I was glad to be out of the house more than usual.

One of the disciplines I benefited from at Pauline's was that she made us cook once a week. Emile and I got to choose a recipe from a magazine, create a budget for the groceries, and cook the meal ourselves. I wouldn't say I am a good cook, but I'd say it taught me the foundations of grocery shopping and cooking. While living with Mom, we went to food banks often. Looking at the prices of different types and brands of cheeses never occurred to me. At the food bank there was one kind of cheese, and it was whatever they offered us.

~ * * * ~

I never felt like I had any special connection with Pauline, but I wanted to be her favorite. I wanted to be everyone's favorite. I wanted to be the most loved by everyone, even if I didn't like them.

Emile definitely created more trouble than me. She'd run away, spent time in jail, and blew up at Pauline often. They'd call each other names and scream at each other, and I stayed quiet. Pauline had to at least enjoy me more, but I needed to be assured she liked me the most. Being loved wasn't enough. I had to be the *most* liked and loved.

Even though Emile was older than me, I had influence over her. I was the leader in our relationship. She looked up to me, but we were also equals and close friends. So when Emile wanted to get into a fight at school, even though I could have persuaded her not to, I encouraged it, which eventually got her suspended. I'll even admit that I liked the drama; but of course, I didn't want to be the direct person who received the attention or consequences of it.

The night Emile wanted to sneak a boy through our window, I didn't stop her (though I think she would have not done it even if I said it was a bad idea). I acted like it would be no big deal and she wouldn't get caught. Then once the boy was in our room, I acted like I had to go to the restroom. Before opening our door, she hushed me and told me to be quiet so I didn't wake up Pauline. But I didn't go to the restroom. I purposely poked Pauline awake, told her to be quiet, and come to our room. When she opened the door, I pointed under my bed where I saw the boy hiding. I wasn't concerned about Emile, her getting pregnant at a young age, or being a young woman of good character. I just wanted to be the favorite.

Pauline yanked the young man from underneath the bed, and I felt satisfied with myself. The police were called, and while Pauline stood over the poor boy in the narrow hallway outside our bedroom, Emile was shamed and blamed. The boy was convicted of trespassing, and now, certainly now, I must have been the favorite.

In the foster care realm, we are good at pointing out trauma when behaviors look like Emile's, but we celebrate when it presents itself as perfect and poised. I had trauma too, but it was hidden, sneaky, and even praised. Just as I didn't really understand the spiritual realities and ramifications of what I did with Jude at the time, Emile probably didn't understand any of that either when it came to the boy hiding under her bed. I hate the shame I felt over a mistake like that. I remember the pain, the regret. And because hurt people hurt people, I couldn't see at the time that I had turned around and inflicted that same pain on Emile. It's not that she should have been in bed with that boy. None of us should have. The problem is that I handled what she was doing in a terribly selfish way so I might gain a little love or favoritism. Trauma is tricky that way.

~ * * * ~

Eventually, Emile left Pauline's. She turned eighteen, and like many eighteen-year-olds in foster care, she wanted out of the system. She craved freedom from the bureaucracy. Pauline tried to reason with her before she turned eighteen and said she'd offer Emile more freedom.

But when Pauline told Emile she could go to the mall unsupervised, Emile never came back.

Emile was really the only good part about being at Pauline's, so I asked my caseworker if I could leave. I said I hated living there. And I think we all knew it wasn't the best fit. While sitting on the couch across from Pauline and my caseworker, we tried to talk it all out, but somewhere in the mess of conversation I could see my caseworker's dismay and defeat. She gestured to me to pack my things and head out.

If there was one thing my caseworkers did right, it was keeping me in the same school district. I was the predicted valedictorian with a 4.0, and I was the fastest leg of a state-qualifying relay. Whenever my caseworkers moved me out of the school district, even just to stay in a temporary home, my teachers and coaches advocated for me, telling them I needed to remain at Tinora High School, so opportunities weren't stripped away from me.

After I left Pauline's, I stayed at two homes for a short time. The first woman lived out of my school district and definitely had more animals in the home than the law allowed, so we knew I couldn't stay there. The second woman had more anxiety than I did on my worst days. She accused me of smoking with the window open every time I went to the bathroom, which then made me anxious to go to the bathroom.

Now I see this foster mom as an adult. Let me tell you, it's weird seeing foster parents who treated and perceived me poorly. Most of them say things like, "Oh, I knew you would do big things!" It is ironic because it was rare that they treated me as if I were going to do anything other than heroin while I was in their home. I know that's not true for all foster parents. But it was true for a lot of mine, including this woman. Thankfully, I didn't stay with her for long before I went to Esperanza and Craig's.

Chapter 13

MOVED

Usually recommend to infertile couples that if they get involved in foster care because they want babies, they should prepare themselves for older children. Many times infertile couples who wish to adopt babies through foster care say yes to placements who are older, hopeful it will work out. Though intentions are sweet, many of them are unprepared for teenage behaviors or reunification, though reunification with the biological family is a large part of the foster care system.

Children aren't products we get to choose for our own convenience. Rather, children are gifts to foster parents to refine their already God-given gifts. The purpose of foster care is not cheap adoption. The purpose of foster care is to make families whole, and while sometimes that happens through adoption, other times it happens through reunification. And many times, it's not with a newborn. If you're going into foster care to fill your own picture-perfect hopes and dreams, you're going into foster care for the wrong reasons. Foster care is solely to fulfill the needs of the most vulnerable families and children in our nation.

Now, many families do go into foster care and adoption to fulfill their own wants, but because God is so kind to us, He aligns our hearts with His. Foster care and adoption can be entered into for selfish reasons, but what a reason for Grace to abound all the more. Truly, this is foster care. God restores families broken apart through reunification. God brings multiple families together to help raise children in foster care. God makes families whole and offers His children a home through adoption.

Reunification is not always the best option, nor is adoption always the best option. The foster care community knows, possibly more than anyone else, that two different feelings and ideas, like joy and sorrow, or gain and loss, can live in the same place. We know tension all too well, so we must not paint adoption or reunification as always good or bad. Restoring families is not black-and-white. It's a beautiful masterpiece of colors unnamed and newly discovered.

Esperanza and Craig should have been better prepared. They couldn't make babies together because of male infertility. So they became foster parents. They wanted to adopt younger children but thought I'd be a sweet exception to their rule because they knew me from running track with Esperanza's son, Asher, who was two years older than me. So I became their first foster care placement.

Asher would live in the house for the summer, and then he would go to college. I didn't have feelings toward him, and he didn't seem to have feelings toward me. But Asher didn't care to follow the rules. It's not like he would get kicked out of the house. And I loved the thrill of breaking the rules. Plus, it was nice to be held and feel accepted, even for a short time.

Asher made clear he wanted no more of a relationship with me than the one we had. Foster siblings during the day and rule breakers at night. That made nighttime something to look forward to. Within my first week at Esperanza and Craig's, we snuck out of the house to go to a party. I was headed into my junior year of high school, and I had never been to a high school party outside of the pool parties the DARE officer's daughter had. To caseworkers, that meant there was not a chance of there being sexual behavior, drugs, or alcohol.

There was plenty of *all of that* at this party. But I wasn't there for that. I just wanted to be around people and make sure Asher got home safe. Because he was there for *that*.

That night Asher ate shrooms as we sat around the bonfire. I realized I couldn't control my emotions for him as much as I would have liked when he made out with another girl in front of me, which I consciously told myself not to care about even though it made me regret our relationship. I said I didn't have feelings for him, not because I didn't but because I didn't want to, because he didn't have feelings for me. I wanted to prove I didn't care about his rejection of me by rejecting him.

Nonetheless, our relationship didn't change despite my regrets because I desperately hoped he would change his mind.

Even though I was sober and of driving age, I still didn't know how to drive. The rules of foster care said I was too much of a liability to have my license before the age of eighteen. So when it was time to leave the party Asher drove me and two other girls he had been with.

Mom had told me often never to ride in a car with anyone who had been under the influence. But I was the only person at the entire party not under the influence, I didn't know how to drive a car, and if we didn't want to get in trouble the next morning for sneaking out, we had to find ourselves back in.

We were fortunate to live in a rural town with enough country roads and people who didn't drive at three in the morning. Though Asher's driving was terrible, and we veered in and out of lanes, we arrived home safely.

~ * * * ~

I looked Craig straight in the eyes and said, "You're not my dad." Then he cried, and refused to speak to me for hours. To be fair, if he had spoken to me, I would have refused to speak to him. I'm not sure why we were arguing. But I remember intentionally hiding away and not wanting to be found.

When he addressed the issue, he told me he'd never heard those words, even from Asher, though he was Craig's stepson. From foster youth, these words were common hearsay. Looking back, I realize these words were probably difficult for him to hear because he desperately wanted to be a biological father, or any kind of father, really. He wanted to attach himself to me because he wanted to be a father in every way, including me perceiving him as my dad.

But parents can't go into foster care to fulfill what is broken and lost in themselves because in foster care the variable foster parents have the least amount of control over is the foster youth, whose trauma has likely left them feeling broken and lost.

Foster care is a place of such redemption for so many. Abandoned children, barren couples (and fruitful ones too, sometimes), and a broken system come together to reflect God's adoption of His children and an Abba, Daddy-like, Fatherly, love we all seek from the time we are born.

But we cannot go into foster care seeking full-fledged healing—as children, as parents, or advocates wanting to redeem our stories. The only factor that will truly and fully heal us from the inside out is believing that God is our Abba—our Daddy, who takes care of us, protects us, and loves us as we are.

Many times I've held the knowledge of God's love in one hand and the idea that earthly means can heal me in my other hand. In my right hand I hold tight onto the truth that God loves, and in my left hand I hold just as tight onto the lie that I am not enough as I am. But here's the truth for all of those who feel that way.

We are all enough. You are enough when you face infertility. You are enough when that adoption falls through. You are enough when the beautiful life you've imagined looks uglier than you've ever seen. You are enough when you react to your triggers. You are enough when you aren't adopted on earth. You are enough because you are adopted in heaven. You are enough because God is enough, and through His Spirit, He makes you enough. You are enough not because of anything you've done or anything you'll ever do. You're enough because God sent His Son, Jesus Christ, to die on the cross, to declare that His enoughness can make it so that you are enough.

~ * * * ~

A group of kids from the city invited me to go tubing with them on the river. Thankfully, Esperanza and Craig knew that I had been isolated for far too long and let me have a lot more freedom than Pauline ever did. I was grateful when they dropped me off, but by evening we were all cold. Riley, a well-mannered boy my age, invited us to soak in the hot tub at his place. Before I could think, everyone quickly grabbed their belongings and made a run for the vehicles.

I didn't want to stay on the river by myself to wait for Esperanza to pick me up. And even if I did, I think the group I was with would have felt bad and stayed there with me, and I didn't want them to have to sit with me, feel bad, or continue to be cold. They weren't aware that I couldn't ride in their vehicles unless they were fingerprinted and provided proof of driver's license and insurance for my caseworker well in advance. Even though everyone knew I was in foster care, I kept those kind of rules to myself because they embarrassed me and made situations sticky. If I texted Craig and Esperanza, they would likely come and pick me up, and my evening with this group of friends—who I'm sure invited me out of pity, but I was so happy to hang out with—would end.

So I hopped in the back of Riley's truck. Once it got dark, everyone decided to go home, and when I called Esperanza and Craig to tell them where I was, they were livid. As soon as I got in the car, Esperanza started screaming at me. Explaining my position felt pointless, so I stared out of the passenger window and tuned her out. I knew she gave me an inch. I knew I took a mile. And it was because I was scared of never getting a centimeter again. At some point my life would go back to friendless isolation, I was sure.

I call it the "freedom phenomenon." I craved freedom and relationship. Especially because I didn't have either of them as much as my peers did. The system's rules kept me isolated and prevented me from having "normal" social interactions. But I perpetuated the cycle of more rules being placed on me when I didn't follow the rules given to me. I found it difficult to follow rules because I was never told if they would ever go away. What I heard was that I was a liability and Mom would sue caseworkers if anything happened to me. If that narrative followed me until I was eighteen, there wasn't any point in following the simplest rules.

~ * * * ~

In 2014, the year I graduated high school and emancipated out of the foster care system, The Strengthening Families Act was signed into law. It supports "normalcy" for youth, especially teens in foster care, and grants foster youth much-needed social freedom and opportunity. Now foster teens should be allowed to attend the social events I rarely could. Friday night football games. Going to friends' houses without everyone in the home having a background check. Obtaining a driver's license at sixteen years old.

According to federal and state law, foster parents are finally able to make the decisions for their youth to participate in "normalcy activities." When making the decisions, foster parents are told to use the "reasonable and prudent parent standard," which is a "standard characterized by careful and sensible parental decisions that maintain a child's health, safety, and best interests while at the same time encouraging the child's emotional and developmental growth."[2]

If I had had this opportunity while in foster care, I would have moved a lot less. I would have had more friends and better social skills. And I definitely wouldn't have been so angry. But the Normalcy Act came too late for me.

~ * * * ~

I was the oldest student on the bus, and I didn't want to be. Since Esperanza and Craig left for work before I got on the bus, they didn't even notice when my friend from school started picking me up.

One morning a text from Craig came across my phone communicating he was home and in his room when she came to pick me up. He knew and I thought he didn't mind. His text message came across like he was joking, which made me relieved.

While I had spent a long time not feeling like I had friends at school, I was grateful for Craig and Esperanza's leniency because I started to form more relationships. Asher had moved out of the home and wasn't a point of focus. My life finally felt more normal. It didn't feel like I was being criminalized.

The rules I broke, my peers were allowed to do without a second thought.

I came home to find out Esperanza wanted me out.

Esperanza wanted babies to snuggle, and Craig wanted a child to call his own. They couldn't risk their foster care license on a teenage girl who was deemed unadoptable and wouldn't follow simple rules. If I was caught by my caseworkers, I wouldn't just be in trouble. Craig and Esperanza would be too. And I didn't want to be the reason they lost their foster care license. I never felt like I was worth more than her chance at adopting children who would call her mommy.

That made four homes in less than four months, and even though Mom and I didn't have regular visits and I was in permanent custody of the state, they told Mom to come and pick me up. Mom said the caseworkers were tired of dealing with me. As I threw my garbage bag in Mom's van, Esperanza threw her suitcase in her Camaro and yelled at Craig as he cried.

Esperanza pointed at me as I got in the car with Mom, "You need to choose between me and *her.*"

Mom's eyes grew wide as I climbed into the car. "What the [expletive], Victoria. Why did she say that?"

"Craig doesn't want me to leave. He wants to keep trying, but Esperanza doesn't want to risk losing her foster care license. She wants me to leave."

"Are you [expletive]-ing him?" Mom asked.

Of course Mom went there, and even though I said no, *we were not doing that,* Mom kept the false rumor spreading. I think if my case-workers had come to pick me up, they would have had to do less work in the long run because another investigation started to determine if Craig and I had an intimate relationship, and I was dropped off at my second group home an hour from my school district.

Chapter 14

VICTIMIZED

The second group home I entered was set up similarly to the first group home I'd been in. Thankfully, since I'd already finished the program once before, I wasn't required to have a point sheet. My caseworker made clear to them I'd only be there for a short time before a "more permanent" placement was found for me.

Natalie was another girl who lived in Esperanza and Craig's neighborhood and had a relationship with Asher. She snuck out with us a time or two, and we connected over having strong feelings for Asher, by being treated poorly by him, and by not having present fathers.

When Natalie came to visit me at the group home, she brought me a prepaid phone I used secretly. Since caseworkers couldn't find me any place to stay, Natalie and I texted back and forth late at night making a plan.

I figured if I took matters into my own hands and found my own placement, it might actually work out. After a couple of weeks, Natalie's mom, Angel, applied to get kinship placement for me, even though we weren't related in any way. I don't know how we pulled it off without getting caught, but it was the first and only time I had a say about where I was going next.

By the time our plan worked, I had missed the first four weeks of my junior year, which sent my grades plummeting. School never came naturally to me as it seemed to for other kids in my honors classes. I worked hard for my 4.0 GPA. But I couldn't catch up on four weeks of assignments plus keep up with current schoolwork. And geometry was the hardest class I'd ever taken. No matter how hard I worked at it, my brain didn't seem to register what I was learning. Becoming valedictorian was no longer in the cards.

There had only been one other time I had felt so defeated by schoolwork. During my freshman year I found an English assignment to be more difficult than usual. I broke down to my English teacher and told her I wasn't going to turn in the assignment. I knew my grade was high enough that I would still receive a B in class even if I didn't hand in the project. She looked at me and said, "That's not happening. I will not let you give up on yourself." As you can imagine, I finished the assignment and received an A on the project and in the class.

In my small town, I'd acquired a bad reputation and was looked down on by plenty of people because of what they heard and assumed about why I was in foster care and why I'd moved around so often. Some of my peers' parents didn't want their children to hang out with me, which inspired me to be valedictorian even more. I wanted to stand on the stage with a microphone and say, "Could I have really been *that* bad and still be up here?" I had to show them they judged me wrongly, and since I wouldn't be valedictorian, I had to prove them wrong another way.

~ * * * ~

For honors English, we read *Atlas Shrugged*, which compelled me to watch hours of videos where Ayn Rand was being interviewed. She appeared to speak her mind, which was unlike most people but a lot like me. She had a harsh tone, yet people listened to her, and I felt I had more similarities to her than any other woman I saw who mothered and cooked and cleaned and knitted and spoke softly. I was a young woman who spoke up and challenged people.

A majority of my classmates were Christians who grew up in middle-class or upper-middle-class homes, but at this point in the spiritual part of my story, I doubted if there was a God at all and had many questions about faith. I'd chosen to be baptized while living in my first group home, and I went to church with foster parents, but I only did so because I thought religious acts would make some God give me a family and a happy life. And when that didn't happen, I couldn't help but wonder, *If God was so loving and good, then why in the world did He allow so much suffering, not just in my life but in others' lives?* Outspokenly, I expressed my atheist beliefs, and when I discovered that Ayn Rand affirmed those ideals, I expressed them more.

Packing lunch was never an option in foster care. Foster youth qualify for free lunches, so it made sense that my foster parents didn't want to spend their money on packed lunches when I could eat at school for free, but most days I simply skipped lunch and then proceeded to eat large dinners at home. Some of the lunches I skipped were spent painting a mural on my English teacher's wall. One of my favorite classes was an art class, where I could choose all of my own projects, so with my art and English teacher's permission, I painted a woman breathing fire, with a Dante's *Inferno* quote coming out of her mouth.

My English teacher, Mr. Clark, could have eaten lunch anywhere else, but I believe he stayed in his classroom while I painted his wall intentionally. We rarely ever talked about anything light, which I appreciated, so I wasn't surprised when we found ourselves on the topic of religion.

"Do you believe in any of that kind of stuff?" he asked

"No," I replied. "It feels like it's just the popular thing to do. Like if the majority of people didn't believe in God, then would people still believe in Him?"

Mr. Clark paused for a long time. I suspected he was looking something up on his computer to prove a point. When I looked up, he finally said, "I don't know."

There was a long pause in our conversation.

I noted that I hadn't heard many, if any, Christians say those three words in response to a question about religion and God. Most Christians preached at me. I know now those people were probably well-intended, big-hearted people wanting me to know the gospel. But at the time, I perceived that kind of preaching as pompous.

I didn't come to any revelation that day, but those skipped lunches in Mr. Clark's classroom became a safe space for me to ask the burning questions the mystery of God and Rand's philosophy conjured up in me. Mr. Clark sometimes said, "Let me look into that," and sometimes he gave me an answer from his own experience, but what he never did was act as if he was better than me because he had the religious answers and knew Jesus, when I didn't.

His humility and lunch-period hospitality compelled me to keep asking questions.

~ * * * ~

Living with Angel was easy. Her rules were reasonable, and she was a good mother figure who somehow managed working two jobs, spending time with her daughters, and taking care of her parents all while being a single parent.

Eventually, Angel's brother, who was a registered sex offender, got out of jail and came to live in the basement. I tried to tell myself I did not have to worry that he was a registered sex offender. It was a statutory charge he received when he was eighteen. And even though he appeared to be a gentleman and never tried to hurt me, I had anxiety about the possibility of his sneaking into my room at night and hurting me. I stopped sleeping so I could defend myself at a moment's notice.

At the same time, I started dating a freshman in college, a friend of Asher's, named Aaron. He was charismatic, and it was easy for him to *captivate* anyone. He asked me to be his girlfriend in the fall by carving, "Will you be my girlfriend?" into a pumpkin. And everyone adored him. For a couple of weeks at least. Until he started disappearing for days on end, asking me for money, and leaving unannounced.

After a long stint of him falling off the face of the earth, I felt a bit neurotic. So I figured out how to log into his email in hopes of finding where he was and what he was doing.

My stomach sank when I came across a Craigslist email where Aaron described himself as a man who could "play any character" and "put on any face." As I continued reading, the same listing named *me* using the pet name Aaron always called me. He described me as "a girl who would do anything to feel loved," "the best purchase you'd ever make," and "so naïve it's cute." I'd never seen anything like this, but I understood that the listing was selling me. Meaning, Aaron wasn't dating me. He was grooming me. He was *trafficking* me. What I had done when I sneaked out in the middle of the night with him and "his classmates" weren't the promises he made about loving me forever. Once again, my value was dwindled to money in a pocket.

This situation was something I have never been open about, unlike the rest of my story. In the moment, I felt like an idiot, devastated, and crushingly ashamed. Months later an actual classmate of Aaron told me he had a few "girlfriends" and "advertised" each of us once he became close to people. For years I blamed myself, and sometimes I still do, because though I do know I was manipulated with lies to do certain sexual acts, I willingly obliged. His promises of buying me a ring, getting married, and never leaving fulfilled the desires of my felt-abandoned heart, and I genuinely believed we'd be together forever if I did what he asked.

I look back now, and I understand why the situation felt so confusing. After years of counseling and working with women who have been exploited, I understand now he was something called a Romeo pimp—a human trafficker who doesn't use physical force or terrorizing behavior to coerce a slave to do his bidding but rather convinces his prey to fall in love with him in order to go along with his schemes. Aaron, by sheer acting and charm, convinced me to fall in love with him and do what became some of the most traumatizing acts of my life.

After signing off of his email, I never chased him again.

Following that experience, I felt so isolated. I couldn't tell anyone what happened because I felt like a large part of it was my own stupidity. I'd been called slanderous names before, and I didn't want that reputation to resurface. I kept my mouth shut. On top of that, I felt isolated again because the rules of the county agency still did not allow me to live a normal teenage lifestyle, which is why I was sneaking out in the middle of the night in the first place. I couldn't do much during the day. After school, I came straight home and stayed there until school the next day, while Natalie went out with friends. I wore sweatpants to school almost every day and felt too tired even to shower. The weekends felt like years. I had no idea at the time that all of this was a result of me being triggered from past experiences of sexual trauma. The language and education revolving around sexual abuse and human trafficking were not available or apparent to me then like it is now. I had no idea what I was going through. I just instinctively minimized a threat by throwing on the sweats and staying awake to protect myself. I lived in a constant state of this whiplash feeling of being both exhausted and on high alert all the time, which led me to take every pill I could find in the house.

I wanted the pain to go away for good, so I lay in bed waiting for the medication to take me. My hands went numb first. Then my entire body tingled and felt like it was floating. My mom would have been heartbroken, but I didn't feel like anyone else would. If anything, in my sleep-deprived and anxious rationale at the time, I was setting people free of the burden of me. No one would have to find another home for me ever again. No one would ever have to be inconvenienced by my living with them. And I didn't have too many friends to miss me.

Natalie shook me awake and forced me to throw up. She sped when she took me to the hospital, but we never told Angel where all the pills went.

Fortunately and unfortunately (depending on the situation), foster youth aren't allowed to live with former felons, so when the caseworkers found out there was a felon living under the roof, I was yanked from the home immediately. I packed my bags after coming home from school. The entire family sat in the living room and cried. I was sad to leave but relieved to have made it out. Years later it came to light that Angel's other daughter was sexually abused by another family member, and chances are I would have eventually become his victim too.

Chapter 15

SUFFERED

Sally said she and Ron accepted the call to take me in because God gave her a dream of them having one more girl in their home before they stopped fostering. In the dream, she remembered that the girl had curly, dark hair like me. So there was no doubt in her mind that I was meant to be theirs.

Sally and Ron were a cool young couple who had a great reputation in our small town. From the outside looking in, they were an impressive set of foster parents. She was a licensed social worker who'd written a children's book about foster care, and he was the treasurer of our town. Together they were known as small-town heroes when they adopted three children, one being a teen young man, the least adopted demographic that comes through the foster care system.

Sally and Ron so badly wanted me to love them and wanted me to genuinely love Jesus. We did devotions at the dinner table every evening. We went to church every Sunday. And every day Sally aimed to have her "quiet time with God."

We bonded over boating and tubing during our weekends at the lake. Homemade pizza nights consisted of much laughter and open conversations. They readily encouraged me in my track and academic endeavors, driving me to practice and helping me enroll in post-secondary classes for the following year. I wanted to take post-secondary courses throughout high school, but my caseworker never let me, believing I wasn't academically ready to take college courses. I highly suspect Sally advocated for me.

Sally and Ron were also young, which made them emotionally attuned enough not to interrogate me about my time at my boyfriend's house when I arrived home, and they understood Twitter lingo.

My boyfriend, Kevin, was a sweet, brown-skinned pastor's kid I'd met while running track. As hard as I could try, I could never think of anything bad to say about him. Our relationship was generally fun and lighthearted. While dating, we had many questions about God, and Kevin encouraged me to go to his stepfather's 3:00 p.m. church service, which was at 3:00 p.m. because his father, Dewain, wanted to reach the people who wouldn't wake up for an earlier service. On most Sundays I spent a minimum of four hours in two church services.

This had a profound influence on my growing faith. I was hearing Scripture, singing moving songs about who God was, and I met many people who had been radically changed because they offered their lives to God.

I wanted to give my life to God too. I wanted Him to change me. I knew I was mean to my classmates and angry at many of the adults in my life. So I started small and gladly made the PowerPoints for Dewain's sermons. But anytime there was a typo or mistake, Dewain announced out loud that it was "the enemy coming against the church." I connected this comment with his continuous urge for me to raise my hands high during worship, despite my reluctance and refusal, and assumed for months that he was referring to me as "the enemy." Kevin clarified he was referring to Satan actually messing up the PowerPoints, and even though Dewain wanted me to raise my hands high, he wouldn't deem me "the enemy" for not doing so.

A woman who sat in a wheelchair came to church every Sunday. Dewain said if the church prayed hard enough the young woman would be able to walk. Dewain would demand we all talk in tongues, and everyone would—except me. I didn't pray at all for the woman because something about the presumption made me uncomfortable.

The entire congregation fervently prayed until Dewain picked the woman up out of her wheelchair and dragged her from the back of the church to the altar declaring a miracle.

I was a young person who already had much skepticism about God, and Dewain's spiritual manipulation only made me feel more skeptical and less compassionate.

Regardless, Kevin remained compassionate. He was like his mother in that way. We had a curfew, which we always cut close. As he sped to prevent my consequences, we occasionally got pulled over. Kevin respectfully addressed the officer. We only found ourselves in trouble once. It was well deserved after sneakily meeting past our curfews while I was grounded. Even though he was a brown boy and I was a youth in foster care, the consequences were mild and fair.

Kevin ate dinner with us often. We sat outside on the patio table my foster dad made out of a wire spool. He was proud of his creation, and because my foster parents were two cool young adults, I felt proud to be theirs.

As my youngest foster brother, Trey, ran across the yard playing with his sister, Sally demanded he put his sweatshirt hood up. We all knew the family pet rottweiler tended toward aggression when anyone put their hoods up. Still, Sally demanded Trey do so, so he did. As he ran across the yard, the dog pounced up, and my foster parents began to laugh. The dog opened his jaw to clench his teeth around my foster brother's shoulder, making my foster parents laugh harder.

Trey laughed too until he started to cry. The rottweiler calmed down when Trey's hoodie fell down, and the family walked into the house. I followed, but Kevin pulled me back. His serious face stunned me because he was rarely upset. His entire essence was comic relief.

"What they are doing is not right," he said.

I shrugged and put on a grin. "It's just a game."

Weeks before the incident with the dog, I told Kevin about my foster brother's consistent problem of peeing the bed. After discovering wet sheets again, Sally became so outraged she forced Trey to sit in the cold porcelain bathtub as she threw insults at him and poured the feces and urine from the tub on his head. She peered into my bedroom and reassured me in a soft tone. "This is the consequence for him peeing the bed. Psychologically it will actually help reverse it." She explained to me that by sitting in his own urine and feces when he was awake, he would grow averse to it when asleep. It sounded legit, and I felt relieved and genuinely wasn't worried for Trey when I remembered that Sally was the licensed social worker and I was not.

Kevin had a superpower where he could speak sternly yet softly at the same time. "Pouring poop on your kids head and making a rottweiler bite him until he is bleeding is abuse." I stared blankly at him, truly dumbfounded by his seriousness. "Tori, you have to tell somebody."

I shook my head. "No, *you* have to tell somebody. You know no one will believe me." And that he didn't argue with.

I'd be eighteen in less than a year, and I thought if I could just not move again, my caseworkers might be a lot less fed up with me. I thought about reporting the abuse many times after that talk with Kevin, but I'd second-guess if what my foster parents did was even abuse. "I'd experienced abuse. Of all people, I knew what abuse was," I convinced myself. "Abuse is hitting and kicking. What they are doing is a natural consequence and just fun games families do. She's the licensed social worker, not me. If anyone knows what she's doing with kids, it's her."

And even if it was abuse, I'd likely be accused of lying again.

Sometimes I feel the caseworkers deemed me a liar from the beginning because they knew there would be abuse in future homes. What better way not to have to investigate abuse and eliminate foster homes than to oppress the truth-telling voice that would report the abuse simply by labeling that voice "liar"?

~ * * * ~

My mom had never shown up for any of my track meets, but when she saw the attention the newspaper had granted our relay team, she showed up for the state championships. Whenever it was predicted I would claim a superior prize, Mom showed up to claim me.

Aware of her cunningness, Mom proudly exclaimed that she had called the school, informed them she was a parent of one of the athletes going to the state track meet, and requested to know where her child was staying. My coaches and teammates' parents were surprised when Mom showed up at the same hotel where we were staying.

Oh, those small-town, big-hearted school secretaries.

Mom wanted to spend time with me in her hotel room, which wouldn't be a big deal because the outside of the room was visible to the center balcony and eating area where the other adults visited. She'd driven two and a half hours. I could give her thirty minutes before dinner. I knew Mom wouldn't physically harm me, and if she chose to get verbally cruel, I'd just walk out.

Once we were in her room, there wasn't much to do, so we awkwardly sat on separate beds. "I got a room with two beds so you could stay in here with me," Mom offered.

My heart sank because I knew her intentions were good.

"We have to stay in our assigned rooms, and I should stay with my relay team."

Mom snapped back quickly. "Actually, you *should stay* with your mother. You *should* not lie about your mom doing drugs and abusing you. You *should* not be so boy crazy! You *should* not tear your family apart with your selfishness!"

I was used to Mom blaming me like this, but still I cried, as I stood up from the bed and moved toward the door. Quickly, Mom hopped in front of me.

Walking toward me, she said, "And if I don't let you leave, are you going to hit me? Everyone knows you hit your mother. You beat up a disabled woman. Does that make you feel tough, Victoria?"

By the time she was done asking questions, I found myself pinned into the corner of the hotel room.

The recurring nightmare I had since entering foster care is the same recurring dream I've had as an adult. I am locked in different locations with Mom as she relentlessly verbally attacks me. I wasn't living the dream. I was living the nightmare.

Somehow I escaped Mom's room crying frantically. One of my track coaches was a policeman, and it was as if he magically ended up on the fifth floor outside of Mom's hotel room. Maybe he realized I was up there and ran up. I'm really unsure, but when he threatened Mom with his badge, I was comforted even though it only made her angrier. I was carried away by my track coaches. By the time moods settled and coaches, parents, and athletes came back together on the first floor, Mom screamed insults from the top of the balcony until she was escorted out by hotel staff.

The following year, coaches and parents were relieved when Mom didn't show up at the hotel.

On my relay team I ran anchor. When I stepped off of the track, I spotted Mom and Allison standing at the finish line outside of the gate. Sally grabbed me before I could step toward Mom. Her hand was wrapped firmly around my arm, "You better not even think about speaking to her! That would be absolutely humiliating to everyone here based on what happened last year."

I didn't completely understand what she meant by that, but I found her controlling tone surprising. I just scrunched my eyebrows, looked up at Sally, and said, "She has my sister. And she drove hours. I have to say something."

"There will be consequences."

"She seems like she's calm and she just wants to say hi."

Sally threatened, "Tori, if you go up to her, I swear . . ."

It's not that I didn't believe Sally would discipline me. But I couldn't walk away from Mom and Allison as if they didn't matter, like so many people walked away from me. I feel this is the biggest blessing foster care has offered me. I know deep pain from mistreatment so I consider treating people in a way that won't cause the same pain. I do think foster care has given me more of a sense about how people feel and how to treat people lovingly. When I meet people and they shake my hand, I keep holding their hand. And before people leave me, I try to remember to tell them that I love them. Foster care gifted me the stamina to stick with people when they are difficult. Foster care has taught me that not everything is what it seems, and people who may appear dangerous usually need someone to take care of them because the people who were supposed to were dangerous themselves. This is what has caused me and my husband to welcome homeless people, birth parents, and foster youth into our home.

I yanked my arm from Sally's grip to walk toward Mom. I wouldn't be forced to choose. My mom was and always would be my mom.

Sally treated me poorly from there on out. During a monthly home visit with my caseworker, Sally criminalized me for going up to Mom and forbade me from having any contact with her, asking my caseworker to request that Mom did not even call the house phone. When I tried to explain to my caseworker that I only visited Mom for approximately sixty seconds to thank her and Allison for coming, Sally screamed at me and demanded I "shut up immediately." Sally appeared increasingly unstable. Her outburst should have been a red flag to my caseworker. My caseworker should have requested to speak with me alone, but she didn't, I am sure, to make her job easier.

The following day, after the home visit, I had planned to go to the movies with Kevin and his family. Right before Kevin's mom was supposed to pick me up for the movie, I sneaked the landline outside, stood on the side of the house, and called my caseworker to report the rottweiler attack and incident in the bathtub with Trey. The plan was that I'd be picked up by Kevin's parents, and since I'd be in a movie, not answering my phone would be expected. The caseworkers would come to Sally's house by surprise, so she couldn't prepare for the investigation. By the time I did get to my phone, the investigation would be over, Sally and Ron would be caught in their corruption, and I'd come back home to pack my belongings and move out.

But minutes after I hung up the phone, Sally swung my bedroom door open. "You aren't going to the movies." I knew that the caseworkers had called and told her I reported the abuse.

"Stay in your room." She demanded.

Sally took her two younger kids to the garage. I'd learned from Mom, who caught boyfriends cheating with recordings, so I recorded the conversation onto my phone as both Sally and Ron briefed their kids about what to say to the investigators. Once I felt like I had enough information, I snuck back to my room.

By the time the cops arrived, the kids were crying, telling the investigators they were scared and never wanted to leave. Sally marched into my room and asked me for my phone. Minutes later, my caseworker called me out of my room and shook her head at me, suggesting I had caused the family to suffer and the children to be afraid.

I whispered, "Look at my phone. I recorded what you need to know!" But the investigation had been over before it even began. The caseworker ignored me and said I was lying.

I walked out of the front door. The cop in the driveway quickly got out of his car. "Where are you going?"

"I'm not staying here." I responded.

My caseworker walked out of the door. "Well, great job, Tori. You did it again."

"Yep," I replied with a smirk. I was apathetic at this point.

It was as if nothing could surprise me. I felt numb and didn't even care when the policeman yanked my arm and gave me the spiel about being under arrest. He pushed me down and put my wrists in cuffs. I wasn't resisting and weighed 106 pounds.

He shoved me into the back of the police car. I sat quietly and watched my foster sister run outside. She cried and placed her cheek on the glass window. Her tears poured down the window as she mouthed, "I'm sorry." In my anger I said out loud, "All you have to do is tell the truth." I thought to myself, *Then neither of us would have to lose another sister.*

Handcuffed, in the back of the police car, I wondered where I'd go next. Every option for a traditional foster home was exhausted at this point. I'd lived with nearly every foster family or their relatives in the county, and my reputation in our small town would continue to be liar.

Chapter 16

PROMISED

At the human services office, the police officer took off my handcuffs and helped me transfer my belongings from his vehicle to the caseworker's. At the top of one of my crates was a bag of white sand. The officer's voice boomed, "What is this?"

"Cocaine," I said plainly. "Would you like to snort it together?"

He looked up at me. "I hope you're joking."

"It is sand. I used it for an art project." I paused as I watched him take some sand out of the bag and press it between his fingers. "I'm not a criminal." But I was used to being criminalized at this point.

After packing my belongings into a different car, I sat for a while in the human services office while my caseworker tried to find a home for me.

Gigi was a stout woman with spiked blonde hair and too many cats. She briefly mentioned the county certified her as a foster parent that evening just so I could move in with her, though she hadn't completed her training hours. Dinner was ready at the table by the time I arrived. The two of us sat as her cats circled our ankles.

"Is anyone else here?" I asked.

"Nope. Just the cats," Gigi said.

"So, I'm your first foster child?"

"Yep."

"Well, I'll be the easiest foster child you will ever have," I looked up and smiled.

She looked up at me with raised eyebrows. Gigi says now she didn't believe me because of the egregious things my case file said about me, but she will tell you now, I was right.

Before I moved to Gigi's, my caseworker finally gave permission for me to take post-secondary classes. Her decision made no sense to me since my grades dropped from missing weeks of school when I lived in my second group home. But it worked out perfectly for me and Gigi since she was in nursing school at the same community college where I'd be attending classes. Some people might say that was God working, aligning our lives, so that I could live with Gigi. But the flame that had been growing in me, that some might have called Faith, had been extinguished.

I'd seen people, who proclaimed such a loving God to their neighbors, abuse their children behind closed doors. To me Christianity was a badge people wore for status or a mask people put on to cover up their worst blemishes. I didn't want any part in it. I wanted to be seen and loved for who I was.

~ * * * ~

Throughout all of the moves, my most consistent adult and mentor was my track coach, Scott Wichman. Over time we grew closer, texting and meeting often, which made caseworkers suspicious. Caseworkers required Gigi to supervise every practice I attended in order to protect all parties of any allegations or accusations. I practiced two hours each day, six days a week, nearly every week. And despite her rigorous nursing education, Gigi made the sacrifice to supervise each practice.

Gigi's willingness to attend each practice was so important because it allowed me to get out of the house and form a strong relationship with a father figure in a single-mother home. It showed me that she didn't view me as a burden. She made a lot of sacrifices for me that other foster parents didn't.

Scott was a terse man, whom most people found intimidating. He walked confidently and stood tall, even with a short stature. What I loved most about him was that he never seemed to care what people said. And he didn't do anything to receive praise. I think I found it so impressive because I cared so much about what everyone said. He had this unshakable confidence to do what he felt was right even when other people thought differently.

Small-town gossip spreads fast, so I knew people were telling him "to wash his hands of me" before I burned him like they perceived I did to my foster parents. But he took the advice as more of a reason to invest. It's like he wanted to prove people wrong alongside me.

He really never said much outside of training logistics and tips, but when he did, I knew to listen, and I knew he meant it.

"I think you could win state." Then he paused for a long time.

"If you do everything I say."

I loved track, but I never thought I could be that successful in it. I just trained extra to get out of the house and be with Scott.

Plus, I had never qualified for the state track meet individually, only on a relay. I also knew the district and region contained some of the most competitive girl sprinters in my division. On the wall where winners pictures were hung at our school, there were only men state champions.

I had plans to go to college, but after attending an orientation day at a smaller college that had offered me some money for athletics and academics, I realized I'd still be in a ton of debt if I went and had questioned if I'd attend at all. But if I won state, I'd earn more scholarship money. Visions of winning state, scholarships, and wearing a college jersey flashed through my mind.

I thought to myself, *I'll just do everything he says, and if I don't win, it'll be his fault.*

It turns out, I did more than what he said. I gravitated toward this narrative of victory, and I wanted to be at the track or in the weight room all the time. During training, when I considered giving up, I'd ask myself, "Would a state champion do that?" Then I'd keep going.

I read books about becoming a better athlete. I strength trained on the days Scott suggested I rest, and I changed my diet from mindless eating to a diet full of superfoods. Through text messages and at practice,

I pestered Scott with the same question almost relentlessly, "Do you still think I can win?" until one day he said, "You have to believe you can win."

I didn't believe in myself, but the love of Gigi and Scott started to make me believe there was Something Bigger I could believe in. I knew I'd falter, and eventually Gigi and Scott would falter too, but I'd heard of a Mad Man named Jesus who never did.

~ * * * ~

My bitterness toward God remained. Especially when church and books referred to Him as a "good Father." I thought if He was such a good Father, then maybe He would have given me one to alleviate my so-called "daddy issues."

Gigi took me to the same church I attended by myself when I lived with Mom, but it seemed different. The pastor started a nonprofit to serve foster families and human-trafficking victims. Leaders of the church openly talked about the need to care for widows and orphans and connected it with foster care. The pastor recognized Orphan Sunday, National Adoption Month, and National Foster Care Month. The associate pastor and many other congregants adopted children. They educated congregants on inclusive language for foster families and acted like being a foster and adoptive family was completely normal. To them it was.

They didn't toot their own horns or seek praise because they were "caring for the needy." Being involved in foster care and adoption was not some "grand calling you must hear from God" to get involved. It was simply a mission field in our backyards that came after salvation and discipleship. Caring for the orphan, the widow, and the destitute, in some capacity, wasn't grandeur. It was just another one of those things God's love compelled people to do at my church.

They didn't even act awkward, standoffish, or overly infatuated with me because I was a foster youth. They treated me like they appeared to treat everyone else.

To raise awareness about the need for foster care and encourage the church to step into this missional space, the pastor asked me to speak on stage alongside Gigi. A couple months later, my church partnered with a nonprofit to hold an awareness event and told me I could make a sign to raise awareness for foster youth. I wrote on the sign "Stop stereotyping me." People said it was intensely powerful, and some even cried when they walked by. The idea that my story and experience could be used for good was planted like a little mustard seed. If I could do that with three words on a sign, what might God be able to do if I shared openly where God had brought me?

Minding my manners and representing myself well were always important to me, not so much because I cared what people thought about me, even though I did, but more so because I was and am representing the foster youth who have come after me, a population of people that is quickly criminalized and stereotyped.

Many times today when I have told people I am a former foster youth, they reply, "Oh, wow! You don't look like a former foster youth! I never would have guessed." People assume that all former foster youth and current foster youth are doomed for a life of homelessness, joblessness, and jail time. I've decided to break these "generational curses," as some might call them, attempting to make the world change their perspective of foster youth.

~ * * * ~

One day at church, after Gigi had cried to me and begged me to open up my heart to her, the youth pastor said something about opening up and not being so closed to what God has for us. I didn't intend to be closed, but I didn't really know how to be open. So when he invited us to come forward for prayer, I walked forward and asked him to pray that I would become more open to the people around me.

Moving forward, I didn't mind as much attending church and reading devotions when Gigi asked. Neither the church nor Gigi was pushy about who and what I needed to be. If anything, I was pushy about what I needed of Gigi. My pursuit of the championship made me high maintenance. I needed running shoes, track spikes, warmer practice clothes, lifting gloves, healthy food, and a lot more. Without a grumble, Gigi got me what I needed to succeed in the sport I loved.

Gigi was unlike my other foster parents in that she never seemed selfish about money, and if she didn't purchase something for me, she explained why, which made it clear to me she wasn't just fostering me to build her bank account.

Gigi cared for me a lot. Though she slept hot and I slept cold, she bought me a space heater for my room. And when we discovered that it turned off after a certain amount of time, Gigi woke up in the middle of the night to sneak in my room and turn it on. She was sacrificial but not overbearing.

She patiently answered my questions about God and church and prayed over our meals, which compelled me to start praying, even though I didn't believe much in whom I was praying to. Praying was more of a superstition, but I thought maybe I could make some kind of deal with God, so I prayed, "If You allow me to win state and get a scholarship to college, I promise I'll give You all the glory." I really wasn't sure what that meant, but it felt like the right thing to say, and I heard something like it in church, so I prayed it every night before I went to bed.

At some point, I started reading the Bible I had received in the juvenile detention center. Why and how I held onto it throughout all the moves, I credit to God, especially because I have never been good at keeping track of my belongings. The stories of people suffering only to become blessings to others and to bring glory to God stood out to me. Job's story was the most compelling to me because he had faith. He hadn't done anything wrong, but God took everything away from Job, only to bless Job with more when he remained faithful. Though I wasn't faithful enough to be considered a Job, I did feel like I related to Job—like maybe family after family was stripped from me because God had something more for me, to bring Himself glory. Then there was Esther, who was an orphan, chosen to be a queen. She could have played the victim and held onto bitterness, but instead she used her voice to save the lives of many.

The words "for such a time as this" stuck with me (Esther 4:14). Along with the words in Genesis 50:20, "You intended to harm me, but God intended it for good to accomplish what is now being done, the saving of many lives." As I learned these Bible stories and more, I slowly started to realize that my suffering could be a gift rather than a curse.

I see now how and why God ordered my foster care placements like He did. In my eleventh home with Sally, I witnessed Christians who proclaimed the name of Jesus but failed to reflect Him in ways that would draw me toward Him. In contrast, Gigi was a woman of God, who proclaimed the name of Jesus, and the way she lived her life drew me toward Him.

Throughout this time of reading Scripture and going to church, I understood that Jesus suffered, and through Jesus's suffering on the cross, God was glorified and His love manifested. I realized that through my suffering in the crosses I bear, God too would be glorified and His love could manifest.

The worst thing that ever happened in the world, Jesus dying on the cross, is the thing that saves me and allows me to understand that God loves me. The worst things that happen to us can open our eyes to how much God loves us.

Compared to many other orphans and Christians who suffer persecution around the world, I understand my suffering is actually little. In my pain I began to understand that God is love and that Christ truly understands our pain, weakness, and suffering more than any person on the planet can. I came to understand suffering only when I came to understand the love of my Abba, and I only understood the love of my Abba as I came to understand suffering.

~ * * * ~

My caseworkers said even when I turned eighteen all rules would stay the same if I remained in extended foster care. I'd still be a ward of the state, so I *still* wouldn't be able to go to friends' houses. I wouldn't be allowed to get my driver's license. I wouldn't be allowed to attend school events outside of track practice and meets.

In church, the congregation sang the song "Good Good Father" by Chris Tomlin. I found myself singing along to the song. An overwhelming sense of clarity came over me. I was not given an earthly father. But I was given a heavenly Father who protected me, planned for me, and loved me better than any earthly father ever could have. Even when I felt alone, I started to hold onto my new found Faith in my Father, my Abba, my heavenly Daddy. Even when I felt alone, I wasn't lonely.

I don't remember my salvation happening in a single powerful moment; rather, I remember many moments of God revealing and speaking. Because I didn't have parents, I felt like I got to know what it meant to fully depend on the Love of God as Abba. I knew what it meant to make my faith my own early on in my walk with Christ.

My skepticism toward God slowly chipped away as I read my Bible more and connected the stories in it to my own. I could see, just as God had written the stories in Scripture, He had written mine. Each foster home was preparing me for the next. I'd been exposed to many different families to observe what I did and did not want in my own family. I'd been protected from drug abuse because of the passion God granted me for track. My mental struggles were minimal compared to my other peers in foster care. I felt guilty, like I had made it while other foster youth didn't have the opportunity. And so I made another promise to God—that I wouldn't waste my suffering and I'd use what He'd given me to give back to others.

As I grew spiritually, something started to change. My sense of purpose widened beyond myself. I was no longer striving in foster care for my own liberation but for the justice and liberation of abused, neglected, and abandoned children. My success was not simply for myself. It was for the foster youth who'd come after me.

~ * * * ~

During a visitation with Mom, just a few days before my eighteenth birthday, Mom took me to get a tattoo of a track shoe and Bible verse. My caseworker grounded me for four weeks by taking away my computer and phone, which solidified my decision to emancipate out of the system the day I turned eighteen.

I loved Gigi, but she had to abide by the policies and rules of the county. That took a toll on our relationship because I grew sneakier and more resentful of all of the unnecessary restraints.

Caseworkers told me if I chose to emancipate the day I turned eighteen I'd lose the financial aid and benefits the government would offer me through the Chafee Fund. My birthday was in February, and though the practice season was going well, I had no idea if I'd be good enough to receive a full-ride scholarship to college. Having the system out of my life was another motivation to earn it rather than depend on a government fund.

I took research into my own hands and discovered that my caseworkers were wrong. The *funds would still be available to me,* and even if I had been adopted after a certain age, I *still* could have received the funds. My caseworkers made it appear like I had to choose between being adopted or money for my education. Then they told me I had to choose between being emancipated out of the foster care system or financial aid for college.

Teachers, coaches, caseworkers, lawyers, and community members knew I was gunning to emancipate on my eighteenth birthday, and all of them reminded me of the saddening statistics of foster care. The chances of my being homeless, not graduating from high school, being jobless, on drugs, and someday imprisoned were high.

But I was oil. I was boiling. Their reminders were simply a match that lit the flame.

It was another opportunity for me to show them they were all wrong. And when God is part of the story, "chances" aren't the dictator anymore. Miracles are.

Chapter 17

FREED

The court case decision was to keep me in foster care because the only other option was for me to leave.

I had seen the juvenile judge in court at least once a year since entering foster care. He wanted what was best for me, and like the other rational adults in the courtroom, he apparently believed allowing me to leave foster care would be setting me up for failure.

I had packed my bags and gotten ready to leave Gigi's the week leading up to my birthday. The caseworkers and lawyers begged me not to leave at midnight before the emergency court case scheduled twelve hours before the clock struck February 4.

I doubted the judge would allow me to leave but had no idea what to expect when a woman judge walked into the room substituting for him. Every adult in the room spoke before me and for me, advocating that I remain in extended foster care. Extended foster care was new at this point and didn't have a lot to offer me other than housing at Gigi's. Now there are stipends for renting an apartment and buying cars, but none of that was available to me.

When I was finally given the opportunity to speak, I begged the judge to allow me to emancipate from the foster care system. I told her I had no interest in drugs or alcohol or sabotaging my life. I just wanted to make friends, hang out with them, run track, and get my license. I cried and admitted that I didn't know where I would go, but I promised I'd be okay. I always was. Though it sounds dramatic now, I told her I didn't know if I could keep going in the foster care system, but if she'd let me out, I'd flourish.

I could feel the shock of the room when she permitted my emancipation. I cried happy tears in disbelief. I had no idea where I'd go next, but I also wasn't worried about it. My caseworkers and lawyers walked out of the courtroom, dismissively wishing me good luck.

Mom sat next to me on the bench inside the exit door and asked me to come live with her. I knew that was the last thing that was best for me. I imagine Gigi took my leave personally because she wouldn't drive me anywhere. I understood, since we'd built a pretty special relationship and she loved me so well. I understood she had to abide by the rules of the county or else she would lose her foster care license. I could only hope she'd understand that I loved her but didn't love the rules of the county.

Kevin was in school, so I called his stepfather, Dewain, and asked him to pick me up. I started living with my boyfriend. I was aware this wasn't a good look, but it felt like the best option I had at the time. Unsurprisingly, Dewain asked me to stop going to my church I went to with Gigi and only attend his church. I refused and told him I'd be happy to attend both churches.

We argued often. He told me I only went to church for the flashy lights. The truth was that for the first time I felt like I loved Jesus, understood the gospel, and was discovering what that looked like for me in daily life. I was starting to imagine how I should live my life in a way that glorified God. Yet he continued with his pushy manipulation about where I should go to church. I felt increasingly uncomfortable each time he tried to anoint me with oil and protect me from the enemy. He picked apart my faith often and told me that I was angry all of the time. I felt happier than ever, and while I probably did have anger in me, his telling me I was angry only made me more angry.

Before leaving Gigi's, while I was still living there, I enjoyed tutoring a third-grade girl in math. I remembered the mom of the girl said if I ever needed anything I could call her. I found her email from the correspondences we had about her daughter's progress, and I reached out. She offered me a big room and a comfy bed in her large basement. But the first night I stayed there, I called Mom because the hives on my body resembled the hives that appeared on hers after she ate soy.

I continued to sleep there for about a week, hoping my body would get used to whatever was causing the irritation. But my hives only got larger and my skin itchier. I was barely sleeping at night. And then one night, Mom picked me up and decided to take me to the hospital. It turned out my body was reacting to black mold in the basement, and when I looked up what I could do to solve the issue, it appeared having mold removed was going to cost a lot of money. I didn't want to be insultive or appear ungrateful, so I told the woman I would be leaving to move in with a friend.

I slept on people's floors, in people's kitchens, and on many couches. One of the apartments I slept in was so cold, I brought a space heater Mom offered me and slept right next to it. As miserable as it sounds, I felt pretty happy. I suppose earthly freedom looks different for everyone. For me, freedom was sharing life and food and beds. I went to friends' houses and had the sleepovers I'd always wanted. No background checks required.

~ * * * ~

Every evening, no matter where I stayed, I did my nightly training exercises, which consisted of planks, one-legged squats, and hip flexor mobility. On my desktop background, I put the times I wanted to run and pictures of potential college logos. I made sure I got at least eight hours of sleep every night. I shot for ten, but because of the inconsistent living arrangements, sleep was the hardest thing to come by.

The spring track season hadn't started yet. Scott told me he still believed I could win state, but I needed to find a consistent place to sleep and eat. The school legalities would not allow me to live with Scott. I understood systems and people so I never asked, but I started to have dinner at Scott's and Tonya's, who lived just a half a mile from Scott. Scott always cooked me something nice. I remember thinking the steak, couscous, and vegetables were fancy. Looking back, they were ordinary. Tonya also ate differently from most people. She shopped in the organic clearance section and ate health foods as much as she could. Their eating made me see that I wasn't as healthy an eater as I thought. Since I was eating whatever food was offered to me, I decided to get on food stamps so I'd be in control of the food I took in. My monthly stipend for food ended up being more than enough and allowed me to shop primarily in the health food section.

Mom had threatened Tonya several times in the past. When I went into foster care, Mom felt Tonya was trying to steal me from her. Understandably, Tonya was scared to allow me to live with her, and I was scared to ask, but I needed to, and Tonya's was the place that felt the most like home. I promised her I wouldn't talk to Mom or tell her where I was staying while I lived there, and after a long sigh and talk with her husband, she said yes.

I'd never trade the time I had with Tonya for anything in the world. Our reunification was a dream come true for me. I watched her minister to teen girls in her home, so full of grace and mercy. She picked girls up from all over town weekly to bring them to her house, serve them a cooked meal, pray over them, and take them to church. I'd ride along with her and listen to her delicate responses to the young women's fears about STDs and various abuses in their homes.

With me Tonya was gentle and encouraging, which were the two attributes I craved.

I remember sitting on her front porch, crying and laying my head on her lap as she rubbed my hair. I don't remember what I was sad over, but I remember her willingness to sit, and the way she rubbed my head was everything I needed from a mom. She even cried with me. The people who aid in healing the most are the ones who sing an anthem that says, "I love you already." Our redemption stories are found in relationships where people love you before they meet you and love you more after they know the depths of you. Find those people and *be* that person who embodies "I love you already."

Tonya viewed me as a blessing as much as I viewed her as a blessing. She shared her hurts and vulnerabilities with me. She presented herself to me in humility, which communicated genuine confidence and strength to me. We learned from each other. Unlike other adults, she did not try to preach to me. She tried to learn from me, and from her example, I learned more and more what a woman of Christ looked like, and who I wanted to be.

In Tonya's home, I slept better and I was loved best.

~ * * * ~

After practice one afternoon Scott drove me to Tonya's. I still hadn't made time to get my driver's license, nor did I have enough money to buy a car. I finally had my permit and drove with Tonya and Mom occasionally, but really wasn't comfortable parallel parking. Occasionally Scott would take me to practice, but I continuously hit the cones, and in Ohio you had to pass a maneuverability test.

I was looking out of the car window when Scott said that he had asked his daughters, Madison and Emma, and they said they would love for me to be a part of the family. "After the track season is over, our home is yours." I'd wondered where I'd come back to for the holidays. I thought I'd happily bounce around from home to home or just stay on campus wherever I went. But having a solid place to come to whenever I needed sounded nice.

As for the family part, I'd heard things like that before from others. I thought to myself, *We will see.*

~ * * * ~

Visualization was a tool I'd learned in one of the sports books I read. The technique instructed athletes to imagine themselves achieving their desired success. It was almost as if I created a video clip in my mind about what I wanted to happen. And I didn't just do it for track races.

During my first track meet of the spring season, I stood at the start line with a freshman from a competing school whom my history teacher said would most definitely beat me. During practices I imagined racing her and winning. As we got into our blocks, I didn't feel threatened or shaken. She hadn't ever raced me, but I'd raced her and won thousands of times in my mind. On top of that, my confidence in God had grown.

I think this consistent peace, combined with my determination and drive, was what allowed me to break records held by some of the most talented sprinters who ever ran in the area. By the state track championships, I'd gone undefeated. Newspapers and television stations covered stories about my experience in foster care, my relationship with Scott, and my unlikely achievements. Opposing coaches and athletes said that I and my talent "came out of nowhere."

I was competing against the defending state champion and other young women who'd already competed in individual races at the state meet, but still I wasn't shaken. I knew God was in control, and I'd done everything I could to control the outcome in terms of training. I was grateful I'd gotten this far, and whether I got first or last, the feeling of gratefulness would not leave me. My track career gave me a father, family, and home. After the races were all over, I knew where I was going.

I had many mixed feelings about Mom not showing up at my senior state track meet. Part of me didn't want the pressure to moderate her or divide my attention up between her and my races. I didn't want her to think she didn't matter, but at the same time, the track meet felt like it belonged to me and Scott. But another part of me knew I was doing something I'd never done before, and I wanted Mom to be there for it. I wanted to share the moment with her more than anyone else because if it wasn't for her, the moment for me wouldn't even exist. If foster care has taught me anything, it is that two different ideas or feelings can live together in a beautiful juxtaposing dance.

Before the first race, the 100-meter dash, I did the same thing I'd done all year before all of my races. I gathered up my competitors. We held hands in a circle, and I prayed out loud, thanking God for the opportunity to be where we were and asking Him that the talent each of us had would point back to His love.

We lined up in our lanes. The gunman made his cues. In track and field, when sprinters get into their blocks, they usually base the timing of their movements off of one another, so they are down in their blocks around the same time. Some coaches say it is best to be the last person in your blocks so you don't get too tight from crouching down for too long. I often felt like this was a game girls tried to play, and I didn't need to play it. I just needed to run, so I did my regular routine, putting myself in blocks first. This is considered a great disadvantage because

I was crouched down longer than anyone else by almost sixty seconds, which causes runners' muscles to tighten.

We heard the boom from the gun, and girls were immediately in front of me. I had the worst start I'd had all year. I came out too slow and stood up too fast. I knew immediately from all of the practice I'd had and the books I'd read, so I reminded myself to relax and keep form. "Relax and keep form," I repeated to myself. In running, form is like what faith is in life. The millisecond your core untightens or you look at the ground, your form breaks down. You slow down significantly, even if others can barely tell. Like our faith, that must remain steadfast looking up to keep Our Core strong, a runner's form is the foundation.

The 100-meter dash is only about twelve seconds for high school girls. There was not enough time to make another mistake, and some would even say there wasn't enough time for me to recover. "Keep form." I repeated in my head. Though the words in my head were mine, I heard Scott's mellow voice speaking them.

I crossed the finish line in first place. The entire crowd roared as I smiled in near disbelief. I closed my eyes and thanked God like I did after every race, but this time I thanked God not just for the victory but for His Victory. I ran up to the fence where Scott stood on the other side and threw my arms over his shoulders. "We did it! We did it!" Tears trickled down my face.

Scott whispered in my ear, "You did it." One of my favorite things about Scott was that he never wanted the credit. He never wanted to be my hero. He wanted me to be my own hero. He didn't want me to depend on him. He wanted me to know he was there, but I was capable and worthy all on my own.

"Now keep it cool. Emotions will drain you. You have three more races to win." I smiled, nodded my head, and turned around to get ready for my next race.

I presume he was telling himself to stay cool. He knew all he had done to get me there. All of the hours sacrificed. The meals cooked. The rides given to and from practice. And the words he had to find, as a quiet man, that spoke power and confidence and encouragement into my very being.

When I stood on top of the podium to receive my fourth first place medal at the state championship track meet, the announcer said I was the fiftieth girl in Ohio to receive four championship titles in one meet. One of the most overwhelming moments of my entire life, until this very day, was when everyone in the stadium stood up to applaud me. The newspaper man asked me how I would explain my success. I felt God gave me the words when I said, "God has made my trials my triumphs."

I'd probably ridden in the back of one of the police cars that escorted our yellow school bus through the parade the town had waiting for my relay, my coaches, and me.

That evening I went home.

To my own room, to my own bed, and to my own dad.

I was surprised when he popped his head into my room.

"I'm happy you're home. I love you. Good night."

It was like when I finally gave my life to my Father in heaven, He gave me a father on earth. I've witnessed this pattern in my life often. When I want something so badly, I hold on too tight. But when I let go, I experience God giving it to me abundantly, better than expected, better than I could have hoped for or even imagined.

~ * * * ~

I was invited to run at an "all-star" meet where I was recruited to attend Ursuline College, a small division 2, all girls, Catholic school, on a full-ride scholarship. The summer before I went to college, Scott and I argued often and loudly. I thought he was unnecessarily particular about having his house clean. Many years later I'd own my own home. Looking back, I now know he was just being a responsible homeowner.

We also argued about how often I was gone. I was rarely ever home. Since track was over, sleep wasn't as much of a concern. I still had no interest in drugs or alcohol, but going to clubs and staying out late with boys became my form of numbing the past pain and trauma. Being between sheets with men who called me beautiful made me believe I had no pain to address. I convinced myself I was just a more "free-spirited" Christian woman.

Scott tried hard to protect me from the guys I was serial dating. Despite my slamming doors in Scott's face and threatening to leave, he always said my room would remain mine and the door would remain open. His forgiveness made our house a home.

Hindsight really is twenty-twenty. I look back and can see the moments it was so evident I was functioning out of a place of fear and insecurity. When Scott dropped me off at college, I felt confident after his hug that everything would be okay. I planned to unpack the rest of my room before the orientation activities, but when Scott turned to leave, I broke down. I said, "Usually when people leave, it's because we don't like each other, but I love you." He promised me he'd pay for my gas money to drive home, and I could come home anytime I wanted.

I regretted not spending more time with Scott over the summer, but even when I went home for holiday breaks and occasional weekends, I couldn't just sit in the living room together as a family. It took time to feel comfortable with the soft intimacy that made us father, daughter, sisters, and family.

Before I changed my last name, Scott asked, "Are you sure you want to change it? You've really made a name for yourself." I replied, "Well, I'll make even more of a name for myself. A better name."

I felt my new life given to Christ called for a new name because Isaiah 62:2 had inspired me: "The nations will see your vindication, and all kings your glory; you will be called by a new name that the mouth of the LORD will bestow." So I changed my name to Victoria Hope Wichman. An adult adoption was too costly at the time, but I wanted something to mark who I was and to whom I belonged.

Days after my name changed, people asked Scott if we had a romantic relationship. The school I'd graduated from pulled him in to have a meeting, and Mom told people I had married him. It felt like no matter how much success I had, people would continually come up with ways to muddy my identity and reputation. In one hand, I held my new name and my identity in Christ, and on the other hand, I held the lies, the voices and whispers that said, "Despite the Truth, despite His love for you, you'll never be good enough for it."

Scott and I struggled to understand each other at times, but still, he was my best friend. He'd come take me out for dinner and ice cream while I was in college and drove hours to cheer me on at track meets. And despite our struggles, he kept coming. I knew he loved me.

I speak so much about sexual struggles and abuse in this book to show you how God loved me despite it and how desperate I was for male validation. Usually how trauma works is that it is passed on from generation to generation—generational trauma. My mom and my mom's mom experienced sexual trauma and struggles. I wanted it to end with me but didn't know how to make it stop. I know now, one thing I needed to heal this trauma was a man to come along and tell me I was more than an object for pleasure.

Scott did that. He always viewed and treated me so purely as his daughter, calling me what he called his own biological daughters, "Sweet heart."

Scott rewrote my identity. Other coaches, teachers, and community members told him to wash his hands of me, affirming once again that I was something dirty. They said I was trouble. But he never saw a troublemaker. He said he saw a girl with very little hope, and a lot of determination, who needed help. He saw me for who I was and where I was at.

He spoke over me a different narrative of truth and victory. His encouragement made the voices of my abusers and neglecters quieter and quieter.

I tried to write this book so carefully because he taught me that every word has so much power. His words. His rewriting of my identity to show me that what God in heaven said about me was also true on earth, changed the trajectory of my life.

So often how we saw others will greatly affect how they see themselves. Because Scott chose to see me more how God saw me than how the majority saw me, I began to see and believe more in myself as God did.

If there's one thing you take away from this book it'd be this: see others and see yourself as God sees you. Strive to understand how God sees you and how he sees others. It will change everything.

~ * * * ~

I always thought I'd walk myself down the aisle. And when I accepted Jesus into my life, I understood that God would be by my side as I walked down the aisle. But then, Scott walked me down the aisle.

When it comes to fathers, I am not without. I have more than one. And I know now, My Father, and Your Father, He fights for us in the unseen so we may know our true identities in Him.

Chapter 18

SCARED

In my first college track meet I came in first place in the 400-meter dash, a race I hadn't run before. I also broke the school record. My college coach, Coach Brown, said I could do even better, but I needed to gain more weight. I went into college weighing 106 pounds. I've always been petite, but my college coach said if I didn't put on some weight, I'd never be the sprinter I had the potential to be. He put me on a weight gainer supplement that made me gain twenty-four pounds in about two weeks. I didn't look unhealthy, just bulky, muscular, and stronger.

Scott advised against the weight gainer and told me that I was naturally smaller, but I viewed him as an inferior high school coach and didn't listen to him. My next meet, I ran slower. And the following meet, I found it harder than ever to run. When I told Coach Brown how I felt, he said I'd gained too much weight and needed to lose it. Never before in my life have I even considered losing weight, but I'd do anything to be better.

This is where my journey with disordered eating began. All I thought about was food. It became another thing that filled my mind, alongside boys, and allowed me to avoid addressing never feeling good enough in foster care, the hurt of not feeling fully accepted, and the ache that came from not feeling worthy. I used to be good enough on the track, but now that wasn't even a place I could expect success. I only felt good, accepted, and pleasing to my audience in-between sheets, so that's where I found myself time and time again.

~ * * * ~

One of my teammates had beef with Coach Brown and reported him to the dean. I'm not sure what or why, but an investigation took place. Each track athlete was being taken in and interviewed by administrators, and our coach was suspended from being around us.

A female assistant coach brought me into her office and asked me how I was feeling about track. When I told her that I thought I had an eating disorder, she gaslighted me, telling me Coach Brown never said I needed to gain or lose weight. She ended by asking if I told the people who were interviewing all of us athletes what I told her. Whatever was happening, the coaches were afraid and trying to control the narrative.

Weeks later we were informed our coach was fired and we were running the rest of the season without one. I took it as an opportunity to transfer colleges. It was truly a God thing since NCAA athletes need permission to "be released" to move colleges. My coach's being fired was an easy out for me to transfer and have the new start I needed.

I was a Christian, but I knew I didn't look like a disciple of Jesus. I reached out to many other division two colleges all over the nation. Most of them were generous and offered me a full-ride scholarship after the initial email I sent.

But I knew I couldn't just go to any college. I'd end up in the same cycle. Every time I left another guy's house I felt worse, but the worse I felt, the more compelled I was toward the false feeling of acceptance. It was the vicious cycle of shame.

I googled "most religious colleges in America." The first one that came up was Brigham Young. I didn't know much about my Christian religion, but after doing some research I didn't think I was Mormon. The second school listed was Hillsdale College.

Scott encouraged me to attend Hillsdale. I struggled with loyalty, feeling like I should follow Coach Brown wherever he went to coach. He was the first coach to offer me a full-ride scholarship and believe in me. But Scott continuously reminded me that I wasn't healthy and Coach Brown had viewed me as a means to an end rather than a person to be taken care of.

I invited Coach Toile, the track coach at Hillsdale, to our home, where I asked an exhaustive list of questions off my computer as if I was interviewing him. He said, "You will fit in very well here. I think you need Hillsdale, and I think Hillsdale needs you." I signed a letter the following week and had the great honor of attending Hillsdale College without ever paying a penny.

~ * * * ~

Stepping onto Hillsdale College campus did not change me like I thought it would. Within the first week I fell right back into the same cycle, and my eating disorder remained. While hooking up with a guy, he ended up actually wanting to date me. When he asked me to be his girlfriend, I looked at him like he was crazy. "I'm not asking you to marry me. Just try this thing out with me. You and me." Commitment gave him the opportunity to leave me, but the game we played before allowed me to lie to him and myself by saying I never had feelings for him in the first place. Fearfully, I said I'd be his girlfriend.

When I told my teammates I was afraid, they told me I didn't have to date him or say yes to being his girlfriend, but I thought this was my only chance at being loved forever. I believed no one would want me because my family upbringing was unattractive and my sexual history deemed impure and undesirable. But every day of our relationship, my unresolved trauma multiplied because I was so afraid he was going to leave me.

~ * * * ~

In the summer of 2016, I interned for the Congressional Coalition of Adoption Institute and The House Majority Whip in Washington D.C. I wrote policy about how to improve foster care and presented it to White House policy staff and congressmen and women. Outwardly, I appeared to be the most successful I'd ever been, but I was eating about five hundred calories a day. I obsessed over the number on the scale, and I didn't connect with my cohorts because I feared if I did it'd involve eating or drinking too much.

I felt God had given me the gift of running, and if I wasn't healthy, I'd be wasting it. My anxiety was the highest it had ever been. I never had to make so many decisions for myself, and I feared not making the best ones.

I also feared what was happening with people at home. Hundreds of miles from my boyfriend and new family, I had nightmares regularly about them announcing to me that they had to leave out of the blue. Despite my best friend, Chelsey, transferring high schools and colleges to run track on the same team as me, I feared her replacing me with another best friend. The nightmares would not cease.

After the final policy presentation, I still had about six days of the internship left, but after a mental breakdown and anxiety attack, I ended up booking a flight home. Chelsey picked me up from the airport, and I visited my boyfriend the next morning. I was shocked to discover my world actually hadn't abandoned me.

Though I was home, the fear of abandonment remained so I pressured my boyfriend to propose. After two years of an unhealthy relationship, he still hadn't asked me to marry him. I began to break down mentally and physically. We sat on the patio of a coffee shop, and he admitted he wasn't ready to propose. Following his announcement, I had my first anxiety attack in which my throat closed, I cried uncontrollably, and I hyperventilated.

About a month later he broke up with me.

This period in my life revealed much to me. I had a lot of unhealed wounds. I had more trauma than I wanted to face. I put myself in counseling. I sat on Tonya's front porch, crying, as she rubbed my face and cried with me. The pain of wanting a mom to hold me and fully approve of who I was, to say I was enough, would never be healed by a man. This was a hard pill to swallow because though I knew it, I still chased the actions that tricked me into thinking otherwise.

On top of all this, parts of my past continually found their way back into my life. Mom reached out to me and told me she had been in contact with Jack again. He was dying of cancer. She said he had loved me since I was a little girl, like a father would have, and asked if I would reach out to him while he was on his deathbed. I texted him and told him I said prayers for him. Within fifteen minutes he asked me if I'd be willing to take nude pictures for a big sum of money. I immediately felt like I was *just* an object of sex even to the old man who I once called "Dad." The last thing he'd ask of me before he died was for me to be an object of sex. I blocked his number, took screenshots of the messages, and sent them to Mom, mostly to show her the quality of men she'd placed in my life time and time again.

Throughout my years at Hillsdale College, and being on a college campus surrounded by ambitious working mothers, professors' wives, and homemakers, I was reminded why I wanted to live a good life in the first place. The professors, their wives, and my coaches' families reminded me of the family I hoped to build. I didn't want to put men like Jack in my children's lives. I wanted to raise my children differently than I had been raised. I didn't want the demons that sang over me to sing over my children or me anymore.

I was taken back to the seventh-grade classroom with Mr. Rodenberger. I wanted to be a good mom.

~ * * * ~

Throughout college I stayed faithful. Though I struggled with sexual sin, my life was God's. I continued to run track because I wanted Him to be glorified. I did not drink in college. I ate healthy and went to bed on time because I felt God had given me the opportunity to run in college, and I didn't want to waste it. I tried my best to watch the way those around me served others and then tried to serve those around me as well as they did because I wanted to serve God. I ran blanket drives for foster youth because I wanted to pour out the love that was poured out to me. I changed my major to Christian studies because I wanted to know more about God. I led my track team Bible study because I wanted others to know more about God.

By no means was I an admirable disciple. But despite my sin and insecurities, God captivated my heart. I knew He'd brought me to where I was.

Every time I went home for the holidays, I was pulled in a million different directions. I needed to visit Scott, my mother figure, my biological mom, my biological sister, and two foster moms. I wanted to show up and love everyone well. I still do this when I go to visit my hometown. It's not so much a balancing act as much as it is a dance, where I step on people's toes. And when I switch partners, I look like I'm not loyal. Despite the trouble, I do it out of love. I want all of them to know they mean something to me. That they are loved.

~ * * * ~

Before my senior year of college, I interned at the church I went to with Gigi. Throughout the internship, my church encouraged me, spoke life into me, and guided me by teaching me how to read my Bible, how to have quiet time with God, how to pray, and how to serve the church. After reading *The Furious Longing of God* in which Brennan Manning says, "Simply do the next thing in love," while emphasizing John 13:34–35, "A new command I give you: Love one another. As I have loved you, so you must love one another. By this everyone will know that you are my disciples, if you love one another," I saw my faith differently. The gift I'd been given was love, and if others saw love in me, they might come to know that love too.

I remembered Sally and Bob. I remembered that they proclaimed Jesus's love in words but then hurt God's beloved children in their deeds. I remembered Gigi, Tonya, and Scott who didn't seem to proclaim God as loudly in word but showed His love more evidently in deeds. And God used their actions and love and sacrifices to bring me to Him—to help me understand that I was fully loved, as I was, as I am. That's what saved me. I wanted others to have that too. I was compelled more than ever to walk out my faith differently. In both word *and* deed, together, telling the truth about God.

Sadly, by my senior year of college, I didn't have a lot of close friends because I'd dedicated my college years to my ex-boyfriend and track. I was an All-American and school record holder, but I felt alone. When I did meet with people and try to show up, I was on my phone making plans for my next meeting and figuring out whom I could serve. I struggled immensely to be present.

A month into my senior year of college, I started dating a handsome man named Jacob, whom I referred to as "man-bun boy" and "boy scout boy," because his man bun was what drew my attention to him and he talked about his wilderness survival class all too often, while introducing me to board games. I played my first game of Scrabble ever with him. Our relationship started off innocent and joyous. Within the first couple of weeks of dating, he sat me down because he wanted me to watch his favorite sermon. It was the first time I'd ever heard of Bob Goff. He said, "Love God. Love people. Do stuff." Jacob said this was his mission. It was mine too. I just didn't have a cute six-word motto to express it. Jacob's passion to love people is what made me fall madly in love with him.

I regretted not investing more into womanly friendships while in college, so even when I started dating Jacob, friendships remained a priority. Unfortunately, many of the friends I'd gained throughout that year did not know how to react when I announced that I was pregnant and I'd be quitting track, giving up my senior year outdoor season. Looking back, I don't think the maltreatment was malicious. I think people just never considered unwed pregnancy as a possibility at our small, conservative Christian college. And to be honest, I wasn't super vulnerable with them about my sexual struggles, yet I was still learning what true Christian transparency and community looked like. In so many areas of life, I was ahead of where a youth in foster care "should" be. But genuine female friendships that love you and know you and hold you accountable and speak the gospel to you and help you live in line with Jesus's teachings? I felt behind in that. The women at that college recoiled from my presence, understandably, but that left me more lonely than ever.

I know Jacob and I stumbled, but regardless of the sin and fear of the repercussions, I never considered abortion. My pro-life values had been refined since the moment I discovered my own mom gave me life in much more adversity than I'd endured. I believed every child should be celebrated and was deeply pained when only a few pro-life Christians said "congratulations" when I informed them I was pregnant. In my pregnancy, I'd suddenly become everything I'd ever wanted: a safe haven and a home. I get that the context of my story meant that the baby had come into the picture outside of God's design of "marriage first," and hear me say this: that's a good, good design. But how was it possible that when I chose life—when I *chose* what the pro-Life movement always wants people to choose—my child was not celebrated as a soul made in God's image? A soul that mattered?

Please, if you are pro-life, expect that you're going to be surprised sometimes—meaning, sometimes the last person you'd ever expect to get pregnant out of wedlock gets pregnant. So practice your reaction to the news a hundred times over because a young and scared mom will not forget the first reactions people had toward her baby, toward her choice for life. Your response of gratefulness for the life of a child and the courage of a mom does not mean you condone sexual immorality. Unwed, pregnant moms likely already know they made a mistake in the sexuality department (and they are likely already carrying a lot of shame about that), and you'll have time to shepherd them in good, biblical sexual choices as you walk forward with them in relationship. But *please,* be happy for life when they choose it. Give them the gift of celebration for offering a future to their child in a world that considers abortion a given and children a nuisance.

I didn't feel fear when I saw the pregnancy test, but my body felt it because I went into the mode I appear to thrive in: survival. I sat in my car and mapped out many different options and plans before heading to tell Jacob at 3:00 a.m.

Jacob and I decided we would wed, and voices said we were only getting married because I was pregnant, when the reality is Jacob had admitted to his closest friends he wanted to marry me before we were pregnant. We were attacked by people in the church. Those voices took a great toll on my heart. I felt like someone asking me to marry him was the closest thing I'd receive to someone on earth choosing me first (aside from Scott's adoption of me). The truth that permeated my mind during our wedding was that the pregnancy forced Jacob to marry me and I still wasn't chosen. The last chance I had to be chosen first, I ruined by getting pregnant.

Thankfully, Jacob has chosen me every day since our wedding. I told him when he proposed that the one thing he could never do was threaten to leave me. Though our marriage has been far from ideal, and we have both thrown mean words to break each other down at certain points, he has kept his side of the deal and has never threatened to leave me.

Chapter 19

LOVED

No one told us we'd have a funeral at our wedding. So many expectations had to die for both of us.

Early on in our marriage, Jacob dealt with depression, and I dealt with anxiety and a need for achievement, which was its own kind of addiction. We had no idea how young we were at this thing called walking with God. But God knew. And He helped us along. Throughout the mistakes and pain, God exposed us and refined us. Thankfully, we both have God, which allows us to be human together.

Most importantly, we've held onto our mission, and we live it out. We talk about it all the time and ask each other how we can love people more. How we can show the Love of God more to others. I believe this is what keeps us close to the Father and keeps us falling in love with each other.

We value hospitality. Nearly every day someone walks into our home unannounced and is fed. We have maintained our guest bedroom despite having six children at one point, and I don't think a week goes by that someone isn't sleeping in it for at least one night. We started a summer internship where a young woman lives with us because I felt living with different people gave me a strong sense of what I wanted out of life. We aim to intentionally host people at our dinner table at least once a week if we are in town. We say our family changes monthly. We have many people who call us family, who aren't related by blood or legal papers, and we wouldn't want it any other way.

At twenty-two we had our firstborn son, Leyonder Edward Amadeus. I know his name is as long as a train, but we loved that his initials would be LEAP, and I needed the meaning "the love of God" to be somewhere in his name. At twenty-three we became certified foster parents and took care of youth in foster care through respite care. At twenty-four we took in a young adult immigrant from Liberia who had been sleeping in public bathrooms. When he came to us, he hadn't even finished his freshman year of high school, but he was supposed to be a senior. By God's grace, we helped him catch up in school and graduate. Months later I birthed our beautiful daughter, Ezzeri Hope, started taking in foster placements, and adopted that Liberian young adult, our son, whom we call Sar. People look at us weirdly when we say we have a young adult adopted son, but I believe when we walk hand in hand with Jesus, people should be looking at us funny because we will experience and live out real-life miracles on earth.

After that, in 2021, I decided to compete in a pageant, for fun really. Track tattooed in me a love for competing, and I credit foster care for making me feel like I have to put myself in new and challenging situations for amusement. Foster care also brought with it so much judgment and scrutiny from other people before they even took a chance to get to know me, so when the opportunity for pageantry came to me, I pulled back on my initial assumption that it was superficial and chose instead to *get to know it first*. In other words, I wanted to give the Mrs. Universe Pageant a try before I dismissed the pageantry industry altogether.

I hired a coach, prepared for about two and half months, and was honored to have won the title of Mrs. Universe. It was the fun I needed at the time that allowed me to not work for God, but have fun with Him. The title was a bonus, and it wasn't me as much as it was Christ in me.

In recent years, I've also gotten involved in ministry and advocacy work to ignite change in the foster care system, and I have witnessed the influence and impact it has all had on children within it. Through my work in these spaces—well, really, Christ's work through me—youth in foster care are discovering that they don't have to fall into the tragedy the world destines for them. None of us do. God has the final say.

People ask us all of the time how we do it all. And I want to say so loud and clear, it has nothing to do with us and everything to do with Jesus.

Jesus in us picks our feet off the ground and sets the fire in our hearts. As for the "how we have time" question, we just rotate the things that go undone. The laundry lays on the bedroom floor at times (like a lot). The book goes unwritten at times. The meals are less nutritious at times. There is no mom shame in my house!

If not the "how" question, we get asked the "why" question a lot. Why do we do all these things? We do all these things because God's love compels us. And even when the world tells us to slow down and shut our doors to the community around us for the sake of our own comfort, we have experienced that the more we open them, the more energy the Holy Spirit gives us for His mission. We do it because people did it for us. I wouldn't welcome people into my home if not for the people who welcomed me. We do it because if God calls you to it, He will see you through it. It may not be cute. He may see you through it in an adverse way you didn't imagine or pray for because that's usually the sanctifying way God draws us closer to Him.

If you want to live this way, let me encourage you: He's got you. All for His glory. All for the sake of love. All for the sake of the others who might know His love and His hospitable arms open wide to them.

~ * * * ~

I treat my foster children's biological mom, Tatiana, like I would want to be treated if my children were taken out of my home and placed in a stranger's care and into a system many deem corrupt and unjust.

My caseworkers didn't understand this. They were uncomfortable when I told them I told Tatiana she was loved by our family and by God. I ended many texts I sent her with, "We are praying for you, and we love you." This sent caseworkers into a tailspin.

Then in April, when we were fostering her children (a sibling group of three), I went to the store and had my biological kids with me (I didn't bring along the others that day). They were sleeping, and I only needed to run inside for something quickly, so I left them in the car. Mothering five children three and under probably wasn't the best yes I've had in my lifetime, but I was afraid that the sibling group would be separated like my sister and I were all those years ago. In this season, I was reminded that decisions had to be made out of faith, not fear, out of conviction and calling, not just a need.

During the short time I was in the store, and while my children were sleeping, the cops were called on me. A week later our three foster children were removed from our home. I made an unwise choice, for sure. I can say that with full transparency, and I regret my actions. At the same time, being treated like a criminal all over again was devastating. I've worked hard not to be on *that* side of the foster care system, but here I am, unable to take in foster children at this time. Though I have been pretty upset about the entire situation at times, I also recognize that the caseworkers are trying their best to do what I wanted my caseworkers to do: assure that children are in safe homes.

Being a safe person is something I've strived for. When it's all said and done, I don't care to be remembered as a powerhouse. I hope to be remembered as a safe house.

At the beginning of 2021, God had set Luke 12:48 heavy on my heart: "Everyone to whom much was given, of him much will be required" (ESV)." I do feel God has given me so much, and I want to do much with all that He has given me. So I asked God to make clear to me what He wanted me to do with this word. The Scripture became heavier and heavier, but I still wasn't sure what "much" God wanted of me. When the foster babies were taken from our home, I realized God had given me much to take care of, and I had much to be responsible for.

Many ministers have broken hearts and have turned people away from the church and the gospel because they do not take good care of what God has given them responsibility over. This reality that I was not responsible in that decision at the store set some much-needed humility in my heart, and though I don't think I'm ready to wave the white flag at being a foster parent, I have accepted that just because I am a survivor does not mean I can do it all. I'm still learning and growing. I've still got areas I need to mature and develop. And God is good to me in all of that, for He is my Shepherd, and He's teaching me little by little. I believe I'll be ready one day, but I have peace that day doesn't have to be today.

Wildly enough, Tatiana and I remain in contact. I still wanted to be a source of encouragement, Love, and Truth in her life, knowing she didn't have many people by her side. During the week of Thanksgiving, she had no one to spend the holidays with. After prayer, my husband and I decided to invite her to Thanksgiving and to let her live with us, in attempts to help her rehabilitate and get her children back in her care.

The pain of letting her down and the idea of inflicting trauma onto her children's brains when they had to be moved to another family after connecting with us wrecked me. But I stand in the Hope of God, seeing that few people are brave enough to care for her children, and even fewer are brave enough to take care of *her*.

Tatiana has spent nearly a decade in institutions and shelters, and she is three years younger than me. When considering if she should come and stay with us, we thought long and hard about the safety of our children. At the same time, we wondered how a person was supposed to learn basic life skills when the only thing her mind and heart could put energy toward is simply surviving. She has no idea what it's like to live in a real home, but we pray by watching us, like I watched Tonya and many foster families, she can learn.

I wondered often how many families would be made whole if there was a foster care support system for birth parents. While I know that God "does not willingly bring affliction or grief to anyone," especially those foster babies, I see again that it is in my struggles that God gently teaches me the most (Lam. 3:33). I see that there are loving families for children, but there aren't loving communities ready to wrap around parents who lose their children.

This is what has compelled us to open our home to this young mom. It is actually easier for me to care for her than it was her three kids. I think that's because I can so easily picture myself as Tatiana. After I emancipated from foster care, my life could have easily looked like hers, and at times it has. The statistics say it still should. The statistics say my biological kids should be in foster care too.

I could be homeless and alone. I could have continued to mix up the feeling of being healed with the feeling of being numb. I could have continued to push away the people who helped me because so many of the people who were supposed to love and help me didn't.

I could have never been exposed to the Truth of the gospel, which tells me that my past sins are paid for and my future is secure, that I don't have to be afraid of my past because I am free from its power over me. From what has been done to me and from what I have done. From all my past sins and coping mechanisms and strategies to gain value or worth from the world. You and I can be made new all because a Madman of Love first loved us.

I treat their mom how I want to be treated, not just because I could have been her, but because, at times, I have been her. But Love overtook me. Love saved the day. Love changed my ways. So I try my best to call upon that Love.

Now that I have my own babies, I hear my mom's cry differently. The cry she cried when I was first taken out of her care, when she had a gun pointed toward her body. She wasn't screaming, "Don't shoot." She was crying, "My baby, my baby." She wasn't worried about the gun that could have killed her. She was worried about me.

Growing up, I'd tell myself I didn't want to be like Mom, but I've accepted that I am much like her. I wrote this book with hopes similar to what my mama had—that maybe I will be able to offer one person a better life than the one I had because of my willingness to write these words even when it was difficult.

I never wanted to accept psychiatric medication because I felt like if I did, then I'd be just as ill as Mom. Mom struggled to work and parent without her medication. But while writing this book, my anxiety became heightened—I assume from the memories. I finally decided to take antianxiety medication, and I feel that it has helped me be a better mom, wife, and disciple. I am more like Mom than my childhood self would have ever liked to admit. I am no better than Mom, but I am also my own self.

Like Mom, I started working for my child. Writing helps me process, and many people say I am good at it, so I initially thought, *This is the way I can bring in money to support my family, while also staying at home.*

Though I know I am not simply destined for the same outcome, it's still scary because I catch myself doing exactly what Mom did, only in different ways.

I've been deeply influenced by Christ in my life. I want to love and serve. I want to offer people a family and home. I want to tell my testimony generously—all because I see it is what God called me to. But before I knew the love of Tonya, Scott, Gigi, and the church and Christ, I knew the love of my mama.

People often ask me, "Do you still have a relationship with your mom?"

I do, and what has helped me continue that relationship, despite my and her worst inclinations, is my hope for her to be saved by the love of Christ. Though I know God is in control, I carry the responsibility of being a reflection of Christ to Mom. I want to return good for evil any chance I get with her because it might just give her a living picture of what Jesus is like. I know the picture can't save her, but it can point to the Masterpiece Maker. On top of that, I know the number one reason people won't associate with the church is because people who proclaim Jesus's name don't act like Him, and I don't want to turn people away from God. I want to turn people toward God *and* His church. And though Mom would identify as a Christian, she won't step foot in a church.

But maybe, just maybe, one day that will change.

I call all my babies what my mom called me: "Baby." It's intimate. It's an image of heaven for me. Of course, I don't know what heaven will be like, but as I've imagined it, even as an adult, I picture God, my Abba, hugging me and holding me in His lap. In a way, it's like being in a mom's belly all over again. No safer place. No better place than with the one who created me in His image, wrapped up tight in His love. He doesn't scream or cry. There's no reason to. Instead He whispers the same words my mom cried, "My baby, my baby."

And I reply, "My Abba, my Abba."

ACKNOWLEDGMENTS

This book was inspired by people who live their lives not just preaching about Jesus but trying their best to act like Him. Even if they weren't mentioned in the pages, I hope they know who they are. They were the ones who inspired me to love. I would have kicked Love to the curb a long time ago if it wasn't for you.

Each of my children were so patient with me in their own ways as I wrote and launched this book. I sat in front of my fireplace for hours on end to prepare this book for the world, not just because I love fireplaces but because I loved being near you, my babies, in the middle of your play area. I hope that this book is for you too. I hope that it shows you how important it is to love the people in front of you, no matter who they are or where they come from.

Jacob, my husband, you sacrificed so much for this mission. Anything I do wouldn't be possible without your willingness to proclaim, "Go and tell!" May men be inspired by your confidence and manhood that is embodied through dying to self and uplifting your bride.

My sisters, Alexandria, Madison, Emma, Layla, Maddie, and Keri, you've filled a hole in my heart that needed to heal. If this book didn't come from a place of healing, it would be destined to hurt people. Thank you for being a part of my healing journey.

Mom, your willingness to put the hardest parts of our stories into the world, even when we don't see every story the same, is incredibly brave. I recently read something that said it takes three generations to write out family trauma. Thank you for doing the work and starting for us.

Tonya, your gentleness and fearlessness to open your home is in me forever.

Austin Wilson, my literary agent, I appreciate you saying no to me the first few times I begged you to be my agent. I realize now I wasn't ready to put this book into the world. I needed to heal and align my character with my message. Sometimes a *no* is the best yes to something else bigger. A book that proclaims Him without an author that strives to reflect His character can do a lot more damage than good.

There are a lot of things that I don't know, but I just want to say thank you to my publisher, B&H, and my editor, Ashley Gorman, for letting me talk about what I do know a bit about: foster care and God. And thanks for letting me pretend I know some other stuff! :) To write a book at the age of twenty-four is really scary, mostly because I know I still have so much to learn, but you guided me through the process with a heart to protect me.

Countless people at Hillsdale College taught me how to ask good questions, the most important question being, "How can I love you?" My education taught me how to write confidently. Brad Birzer, when you told me that one of my Instagram posts was the best piece you'd read in years with tears in your eyes, I knew I was meant to write. My education was invaluable. I cannot thank Hillsdale College enough.

To the current and former foster youth, and anyone who has experienced abuse, I love you. You are my reason, and you are so loved. What is a book if it isn't for someone? This is for you.

I've had the honor of working with many nonprofits and ministries. One of the most impactful being the Global Leadership Summit. You sure do know how to pick speakers to declare life over people. When I came to my first GLS, my heart felt dead inside. God used your ministry to bring this mission back to life. When I was barely walking, y'all granted me the energy to start sprinting.

There are so many authors I will never meet who have mentored me through the pages of their own books. Thank you.

Thank you to my tribe on social media who always said, "You should write a book!" No way I would write like I do now or give these pages to anyone to read if it wasn't for your stories of redemption, triumph, and salvation, all because I chose to be vulnerable with mine.

To the broken parts of the foster care system, to my transgressors, and to my abusers, you've taught me what not to be, and for that I am grateful. I love you, too.

And for all those who have taken the time to invest in this book in any way, who have read to this point, I love you already.

NOTES

1. Teresa Wiltz, "Giving Group Homes a 21st Century Makeover," Pew Charitable Trusts, June 14, 2018, accessed January 27, 2022, https://www.pewtrusts.org/en/research-and-analysis/blogs/stateline/2.

2. "Normalcy for Youth in Foster Care," Child Welfare Information Gateway, accessed January 31, 2022, https://www.childwelfare.gov/topics/outofhome/resources-foster-families/parenting/normalcy.